CONFESSIONS OF A SOFTWARE TECHIE

The Surprising Truth About Things That Really Matter

Ramakrishna Reddy

DEDICATION

To my dad Narayana Reddy, for believing and getting me into this world even after three daughters

ALSO BY RAMAKRISHNA REDDY

Connect Using Humor and Story

Toastmaster's Secret

Public Speaking Essentials

Public Speaking Topic Secrets

The Ultimate Public Speaking Survival Guide

TABLE OF CONTENTS

INTRODUCTION

A few years ago, I got into my car to leave my apartment. I had already not slept properly because the production beeper buzzed twice. As I plugged the key inside my grey Hyundai Elantra, my teammate from India called me. I stopped the car ignition, answered the phone, and guided him on further steps to solve the issue.

I started the car, drove through Cold Spring Road, went inside Dunkin' Donuts drive-through in the town of Rocky Hill, came out with a bagel and a cappuccino, raced through I-91, and parked my car in the Atrium parking lot of the Aetna headquarters in Hartford, Connecticut.

I put on my woolen coat, walked through the hallway, and flashed my ID card at the building entrance. The door opened wide and I walked inside the Atrium building. I took the elevator, got out at the third floor, walked up to my cubicle, and plugged in my laptop at the workstation.

I switched on the laptop and opened my Outlook email client to sift through my inbox that contained loads of emails and meeting invites. I opened up my mainframe terminal, checked the job scheduler, and confirmed whether there were no adverse impacts because of the production issue.

I had four meetings for the day: requirements discussion with business team, design walk-through with project team, status meeting for projects, and solution discussion with architect. In addition, I had an instant message from my client manager, "Why did the production issue happen?" To which I replied, "The input data to our application had bad data. We are working on it. Will keep you updated."

I was lying.

The truth—we did not handle a condition from the upstream, when we installed a new functionality the previous month.

My job: tech lead for software applications that generate millions of dollars in revenue. I was responsible for requirements discussion, design, enhancements, business queries, handling issues, meeting deadlines, implementation and warranty of code installation, and production support. It might seem like a lot. And that's why there was a team of seven who were sitting in India, working under my direction.

Essentially, I was the go-to guy for anything and everything related to these sets of software applications. Years ago, the work that these software applications were trying to accomplish would have been mere manual tasks for business folks at Aetna. Now that software applications have been developed, business folks need the help of techies like me to run the show.

At the core of my job, I am the bridge between the software application and the business. That sounds simple. It's not. Here's the reality.

I worked for a software services company. Aetna was a client for us. I was responsible for five different business applications that belonged to our client, which had three different managers. I needed to keep my client managers happy. I needed to keep my employer happy. I needed to keep the client business users happy.

And to top it, I needed to keep a harmonious relationship with veteran techies of our client, and I also needed to keep an edge with competing techies who belonged to other software services companies. But this is not what I thought it would be like to be a software techie. I had a very different idea.

How did I end up there?

I was sitting in the huge auditorium waiting for the results of my campus interview. The air conditioner could not stop my sweat. Fears of failure were gripping my heart. Already, the first company had rejected me after the second round. The second company had rejected me after the first round. I remember that moment when I started thinking about my childhood.

When I was in my seventh grade, my mom used to say, "When you grow up, don't become like your dad." My dad was an electrical contractor for Alstom India. Most of the time, he was away from home because of the nature of his work. She supported my dad but wished a different life for me.

My mom was the best thing that happened in my life. Her lap was the coziest place I have ever been. Her smile was the sweetest sight I have ever seen. She used to say, "When you grow up, you work with computers. You keep hitting the computer keyboard and money should keep falling in your bank account." Externally, I used to laugh it off. But, internally, I used to feel, "Wow, this seems to be cool."

I was born in Chennai. This is the city where Google's current CEO, Sundar Pichai, grew up. I was in ninth grade when I was introduced to programming. My computer teacher was so awesome that he directly wrote the programs on the board. I did not understand a thing.

However, his way of conducting the hands-on exam calmed me down. He was going to test us with one of the programs discussed during regular class. I thought of a brilliant plan—during the exam, retrieve and execute the working program. Sounded perfect. The exam started.

I was so dumb that I could not even locate the folder where I had saved the working code. When my computer teacher came to examine my output, I had to run the code that I wrote during the exam. I just got 32 errors.

I still remember that day when I felt, "Rama, you are going to suck at this."

But I was not dumb either. I was among the top rank holders of my class. The thought of how I was going to have any chance in programing used to nag me. So, I did what most people hesitate to do.

I asked for help, but not from my classmates. Pride stopped me. Instead, I went to my sister Lakshmi, who was the first member in our family to enter the computer field. Seeing her carry thick books with subjects such as C, C++, Java, should ideally have been inspiring. But it was overwhelming. I still have this feeling towards books having 400-plus pages.

My sister was very methodical. I distinctly remember the first time she used the words "algorithm" and "pseudocode." For some reason, the words captured my attention. It was fascinating. *Al-go-rithm. Pseu-do-code.* Rather than asking what pseudocode was, I remember asking her why it was not pronounced with a *p* sound. Without responding to my brilliant question, she diverted my attention to something else. She taught something called logic. Now, the program that I sucked at suddenly seemed to make sense.

She and my other sisters—Indumathy and Leelavathy—made sure I did well enough in my high school to get into a good college, even though my mom passed away because of a serious illness.

I entered Anna University in Guindy campus, Chennai. The campus has a reputation for attracting the best students and hence the best companies for job placements.

During my college life, I had got a glimpse of corporate life—which I realize now. Though, none of the insight came from my college. It came from my dad.

As a teenager, I wanted money for partying, and flirting. My dad did not give me any money but he gave me a lot of value. He taught me the golden rule of life.

Do you know what the golden rule is? Hurt no one so that no one hurts you... NO.

My dad's rule was: *the one who has the gold, makes the rule*. My conversations with my dad would go as follows.

Me: "Dad, can you buy me a motorcycle?"

Dad: "No."

Me: "Can I go for an overnight party?"

Dad: "No."

Me: "Can you at least buy me a cell phone?"

Dad: "No."

Dad: "No."

Me: "I did not even say anything."

Apparently, my dad had equipped me for the harsh realities of the *real* world. And the road to enter the real world came in the form of campus placements during my final year of college.

In India, the software services sector was growing like crazy. Companies were fighting to get the first slots for campus placements. They seemed like the big bad guys grabbing innocent college kids and loading their trucks on a first come, first serve basis.

I cleared the written test for the first company. I did well in the second round too, but the interviewer did not feel so. I wrote the first round for the second company. I was not even shortlisted.

Then, it was the turn of the third company. The first round was a written test. There were two parts—one part had 10 puzzles to solve, but I attempted only four; the second part was about English proficiency, which went decently.

I lost hope because all my friends seemed to do well. To ease my depressing mood, I went home—which takes a few hours to reach by public transport—and started watching the movie *Road Trip*. At around 7 p.m., my dad came inside my room saying, "Your friend called. It seems you have an interview at 8 p.m."

The first thing I remember is closing the Windows media player so that my dad did not notice the scene I was watching to make myself happy.

The next thing I remember is my dad driving his car like a hero galloping a horse. We finally reached the interview center at 7:50 p.m.

One friend changed my shirt. The other friend tied my tie. And finally I attended the interview.

The next day, I was sitting in the huge auditorium waiting for the results. They started announcing the results: 50 gone, 100 gone, and 120 gone. My name was not there. Feelings of failure filled my heart with fear until I heard "127 Ramakrishna Reddy." And thus, I got the ticket to become a techie.

Over the past 11 years, I have been working from locations across India as well the United States as a developer, technology analyst, technology lead, business analyst, project manager, scrum master, or any of the several other fancy labels out there.

Sometimes, even I am not sure on the role I am doing. During this time, there have been certain things I should have done, and certain things I shouldn't have done. Currently, there is disruption in the tech world. Yes, the disruption is real but not as exaggerated as it is showcased. If you are not ready to make changes to tackle this disruption, you cannot blame anyone but you.

Technology is changing things at supersonic speed, and techies are at the forefront of this shift. Yet no one seems to be talking about things that really matter in work, life, and beyond.

My examples and data points often focus on guy techies working in the United States and India, for the simple reason that I am a guy and have worked in these two countries.

However, the essence of this book should help even techies who are girls, techies in other countries, and any corporate professional at large. Trust me, if nothing else, it won't be boring.

I might have polarized views, but I give reasons for the same. I have made my best effort to keep the substance useful from a holistic standpoint, addressing both work and life, which is the whole point of why we do what we do.

I believe learning to program life is more important than learning any programming language and it is my sincere wish that you reprogram your life with the information in this book.

So let's get started.

—Rama

PART 1

The things that matter in Professional life

CHAPTER 1

TEN LESSONS NOT TAUGHT IN CLASSROOMS

In which, we'll see sales, programming, ownership, failure, honesty, ego, loyalty, perception, comfort zone, and performance in a counterintuitive way

When I was in school, my friend asked me, "How is differential calculus going to help me in life?" And I used to think, "How does it matter? Our job is to study and score marks."

Deep down, even I did not know the answer. Now that I have spent more than a decade as a techie, I can certainly tell that I haven't used differential calculus. And I am sure that except for folks in research areas, no major workforce will use differential calculus. Moreover, I haven't used a plethora of concepts that I learned in high school. That does not mean we should not go to high school or college.

High schools and colleges teach us to: be competitive (you make a personal decision to prove yourself when you get a lower rank or mark than that other guy or girl), do boring stuff (studying and practicing for exams), help others (teaching classmates complex topics), work in teams (the group study where you actually studied), handle last-minute pressure (cramming on the night before the exam), and a lot more things.

But, there are certain things that I learned only after being a techie. If given a chance to reform the education system, I'd add the following points as lessons in schools because everyone needs to understand the work world, which is kind of the "real" world.

You are in the sales business

Though there are many different business models in the tech world, as a techie, you'll encounter only two kinds of environments.

Type one environment is where we service customized software applications that automate the organization's business logic. Type two environments involve commodity software applications that can be sold as a product to other companies or consumers.

The environments are getting more complex day by day. In the type one environment, the organization (usually called the client) that owns the business software applications can directly employ techies (usually called the in-house IT) or contract with a supplier (usually a service-based tech company). The trend is to have less direct employees and more contractual techies. Almost all the service-based tech companies—Capgemini, Cognizant, Accenture, Tata Consultancy, Infosys, and others—make most of their money by supplying techies to service (build, design, operate, maintain) software applications.

In type two environments, the organization that owns the commodity software applications has more direct techies and less contractual techies. The strategy is based on criticality. The direct techies do the critical work and leave the non-critical work to contractual techies. Almost all the product-based tech companies—Apple, Microsoft, Google, Oracle, SAP, and others—make most of their money by selling their software products to either consumers or other businesses.

You might ask why I say "you are in the sales business" when there are dedicated sales teams for the employer. The dedicated sales team is responsible for selling the products or services of the employer. The question is:

Who is going to keep selling you, the employee?

Unfortunately, it's only you and that's why you are in the sales business. Still don't believe that you are in sales? If you are already an employee, you have already made your first sale.

That's right. It was your job interview. What do you think the interviewer was doing? The interviewer was checking whether you were the right product that fits the need of the company.

Isn't that the essence of sales?

"I have always said that everyone is in sales. Maybe you don't hold the title of salesperson, but if the business you are in requires you to deal with people, you, my friend, are in sales," said the legendary author, salesman, and motivational speaker Zig Ziglar.

Selling has a bad rap. Imagine the age-old scenario of the used car salesman. Suppose a man walks in and browses through a used car lot. Rather than focusing on his needs, the salesman starts off pitching the car the customer is eyeing.

We cannot blame the salesman because he only has a few minutes of the customer's attention. But, the prospect knows that he is being sold and wants to run out of the lot. This can be seen in a lot of places and hence the bad rap of selling.

However, as techies we have an opportunity to hold the flag of righteousness for selling, because selling essentially boils down to solving problems, which is what we'll see next.

You are not hired for programming

During a weekly status meeting, I was talking about one problem after the other to Randy Pence, my client manager. I had an attitude of these-problems-never-end. He looked at me in a pensive mood. In a husky voice like Vito Corleone in *Godfather I*, he said, "Rama, you know, if problems are not there, we won't have jobs." Not knowing what to do, I forced a sheepish smile onto my face.

Up to that point, I used to think, "Why am I not free? When will I get rid of the problems and work in peace?" But, when I reflected on Randy's statement, it seemed as though he just enlightened me.

I was so naive not to understand that the very reason I was getting paid was to solve problems. The more I thought about it, the more I believed that he was right. And Infosys was right when they asked candidates to solve puzzles in their first round of interview. They were looking to hire good problem solvers, and they knew problem solvers could be taught programming along with other skills. (Currently, Infosys is not using puzzles during assessments. Maybe it's to avoid manual correction, which becomes impossible in large-scale recruitments.)

I can vouch that you will spend a minor portion of time in programming and a major portion of time trying to solve problems. If your company is small, you'll spend more time programming. However, if your company is big, you might do less programming, sometimes no programming at all. But, irrespective of company size, if you know that you are a problem solver, you'll do well.

You should not be concerned when there are problems. In fact, you should be concerned when there are no problems to solve.

Technology helps businesses solve real problems. And we belonging to the technology side should first be problem solvers, then leverage programming for the same.

You are an owner

Balaji Kalamani is a techie working at Amazon in Seattle. He works in a truly international team with folks from different parts of the world. "I interview at least one person per week," said Balaji. "Within a few minutes, I'll be able to tell if the person takes ownership or not."

He said that the #1 skill that he is looking for when he is interviewing is *ownership*. When he hears potential candidates say, "It was his job to do it" or "There was something wrong with my team" or "This was the problem and they were not trying to fix it," he feels that they are self-sabotaging their chances of cracking the interview.

When you are a techie, you wear different hats such as developer, tester, lead, architect, manager, or analyst. Sometimes you need to wear multiple hats. And that's not when you say, "It's not my job."

In his book *The Question Behind the Question*, John G. Miller beautifully wrote, "Ownership: A commitment of the head, heart, and hands to fix the problem and never again affix the blame."

Some feel that it's just a job and let us be smart by catching low-hanging fruits. I confess that I used to be one of them. But, I truly realized the meaning of job satisfaction only when I took ownership of my work.

There is an absolute pleasure in treating our work this way. When we feel like the owner of our work, we'll do what it takes to get the work done. Ownership is the secret fuel to produce good quality work. That's why you should not be surprised when you see some folks get things done even if they do not know about the technology, or domain. Deep down, even you know this, but I am calling it out.

However, there is a flip side to ownership when it comes to material things. We'll see that in the next to last chapter.

Failure is not an option

When growing up, I often heard the maxim, "Failure is the stepping stone for success." I felt good about this quote because I thought that I would be covered when I fail. All through life, we hear such maxims, yet the reality is totally different at work, where we spend the major portion of our waking life.

Mistakes cost a lot in the tech world. Yes, there are processes and tools to catch them but still they occur. Is it a big deal when you miss a comma or a period in your code? It is.

Let's say a million users use an application. And one of the most used features is no longer usable because of the buggy code. After this mess, can you tell the client, "Failures are but mileposts on the road to success"?

Your client will put a gun to your head.

No wonder companies stigmatize code defects. Nobody talks about handling failure. I am not talking about failing exams. I am just talking about failure in general.

A company is giving top-notch training to fresh college graduates and the company policy says, "We'll fire you if you do not clear the assessment after the training." Imagine the emotional baggage, the insult, and the tag that these graduates will carry if they fail to clear the exam.

I have seen extreme cases where folks take their own lives. Who are we supposed to blame for such dire consequences?[1] When folks failed, do you think parents and friends might have said, "In order to succeed, you must fail so you know what to do better the next time"?

Maybe some did. Maybe some did not. But the fact is that folks are not ready for such a do-or-die scenario. Failure is not an option in the "real" world.

Honesty is not always the best policy

My parents, teachers, and others always told me that *honesty is the best policy*. I always believed it. As a techie in the corporate world, however, I feel honesty is not always the best policy. I am not telling you to be dishonest. I am just telling you that being honest in its purest form in today's complex work culture might get you into trouble. Something else is the best policy. I'll come to it soon.

Let us take a scenario. A CMMI (Capability Maturity Model Integration) audit is approaching. Sheth, a manager, asks Tom, his subordinate, to take care of the audit. Tom checks the situation and says, "No proper documentation is present. None of the process is in place. We are going to be rated down."

Sheth calls Harry, his other subordinate, and says, "Please take care of this." Harry checks the status of the project against the CMMI quality checklist. He quickly creates, and asks extended team members to create, the missing documentation; gets all necessary approvals; and makes sure things look good just before the audit.

Is Harry being honest here? Would you condemn what Harry did? I won't.

Harry figured out a way to deal with the situation and get the work done. If he was honest, the audit would fail. That would be more work for everyone else, which is useless for anyone per se. Instead, the team could spend more time working on other practical problems or work on things that add value. I am not saying that you should not be honest. I am saying that it's okay if you are not, in situations which are nonproductive and useless.

But, I highly recommend that you develop the other trait: integrity.

Integrity is being true to your core values. I find this quality to be lacking or not being taught properly. You show integrity when you say that things will be done and you get them done, whether someone is watching you or not. Integrity is sticking to a set of core values and beliefs about what is the larger good. You beg, fight, or barter, but if you can keep your word, people will love working with you.

Ego is your enemy

Once you learn your craft well, you become an SME (subject matter expert). Your value will eventually become high. And, something deadly will happen.

You develop truckloads of ego. A little success is enough to create ego. If you are not yet there, it will eventually happen. Once we become fluent with something, we run a high risk of becoming arrogant.

I confess that I acted arrogantly with my managers, when I shouldn't have. I confronted my senior management based on rumors, when I shouldn't have. I demanded high-quality work from my juniors without being courteous, when I shouldn't have.

The sad reality is we are replaceable, we are not the smartest, and we don't know everything.

There is always a smarter person out there. There is always something that we'll eventually have to learn. Just because we became an expert in some domain or technology, should not warrant us to develop ego.

Once, there was a huge uproar in the company because of the salary structure. During one of our regular town halls, the unit head said that the company was planning to release the revised pay structure. I raised my hand and said in a cocky voice, "This is great. I had arguments with my managers about this very point. I am surprised that my managers did not know about this initiative."

Everyone in the audience laughed. I got attention and I became famous in the company. Six months down the line, what happened during the performance cycle? I got the third level rating. That rating is really poor. My immediate manager spilled the beans that the town hall incident became the deciding factor for the management giving me such a low rating. *He told me not to quote him. I kept my word by not quoting him but told the truth in a book!*

All the work I had done did not matter. I was the only one managing the portfolio for five different business applications, working under three different client managers. Even so, I was penalized. Nobody even thought if there was a point. The first thought was like, "How dare he speak like that?"

That's what ego did for me. It made me speak like a "righteous" hero, which is a strict NO at work. Take that path only if you have decided to move out of the company and you don't need any damn thing.

The best path is not to channelize your energy towards your egoistic instincts. It's not worth it. I'll tell you later what is worth it and where you can channelize your energy. I laugh when I see some techies behave as if they have conquered the world. People who run successful companies, who write *New York Times* bestselling books, do larger-than-life things still seem to be humble and down-to-earth.

I have found that instead of building ego, *building rapport* creates a win-win situation.

In the past three years, I kept building rapport—not just with my boss or clients but also with my peers and subordinates. If you have rapport, people are ready to go out of their way when you need help. With rapport, life becomes easier (we will see how in the next chapter). Nobody is obligated to bend to your ego. But, they'll bend if you have built a rapport. It just helps like crazy.

Sticking longer is not loyalty

During my assignment with Aetna, the Aetna leadership decided to let go veteran employees—including business and techies—who had worked there for 30 to 40 years.[2]

I always pondered, "Nobody in the world can beat these folks with their competence. They know the ins and outs of the application. Why would a company take such a drastic step? Were they expensive to maintain? Or did the outsourcing prove to be cost-effective?"

What loyalty did the company show to these loyal employees?

In my recent assignment with American Express, around seven people from our employer were part of a larger team. The folks from our team had solid experience in the application. Yet American Express (our client) did not renew the contract. That is a lot of wasted experience. Even at Aetna, there was a lot of valuable experience that was wasted.

Is that experience really a waste? Maybe, yes.

If folks are happy doing the same job, for the same employer, for the rest of their life, thinking that they are building loyalty with the employer, it's time to think again. I really don't think employers need such a workforce anymore. This might have worked decades ago, but I don't see it working now.

Yes, there are employers who value loyalty. And to a certain extent, it matters. But just sticking with an employer and expecting your job to be secure will be naive. When the employer wants to cut costs, your loyalty will not matter a dime. I am not saying that you should change your job immediately. I just want you to be aware.

So what will make your employers loyal to you? The new loyalty comes from giving a value-add—revenue, client delight, or workplace improvement—to the employer.

What matters is how much money you can earn or save for your employer, how you can deliver quality products and services with less expense, and how much work you can complete with minimum resources.

When you do any of these things, your employer will always be loyal to you.

Perception matters

What are you doing right now? You might be reading a physical copy of this book or reading a digital version of this book. Just do a simple exercise. Transfer your spirit and sense into a person next to you. And see yourself from that person's perspective.

It might be hard to do this, but try it anyway.

Do you see yourself reading this book? Do you see the outfit you are wearing? Does it feel different?

You should be able to see in a whole new perspective.

I have an interest to compete in speech contests. One powerful technique to get better is to record our own speech videos and then look for areas for improvement.

I would watch the video and quickly realize, "This is not how I thought I gave the speech." It was painful to watch because I thought I gave the most stellar speech but the reality was so different. My perspective of how I gave the speech changed.

How does this matter to your work as a techie? It matters.

Do you ever see yourself from the other—boss, colleague, client, or subordinate—person's view? The way you dress, the way you talk, the way you respond, the way you ask for help, the way you respond to criticism.

Imagine someone video recording every action of yours. And you see the videos. Do you think you would have the same perspective about how you dress, talk, respond, or behave, after watching the video? I am sure it would be different.

Perception here refers to what others see and think about us. It does not matter what we think—"I'm a hot-shot guy slogging for hours and hours"—about ourselves, what matters is how others think—"he seems to be a loser who is not able to complete work in allotted time"—about us.

In fact, we might not even know how others are seeing us. And that's why we need to know how to handle people, how to get more done with less, and how to communicate properly, which we'll see in the following chapters.

Comfort zone is a bad place

Since my childhood, almost everyone including parents and teach-ers told me, "Study well, get a good job, and you'll be settled for life." What I comprehended out of this was: I'll study hard, get good grades, and work for a multinational so that my life will be comfort-able.

And this is what I see most of the techies do. We chase comfort.

Think about it. How many decisions do we make because they are comfortable? Psyche syncs with comfort. We seek comfort and I am no different.

For the first eight years of my career, I was working with the same team and software applications. I was getting promoted regularly for the first five years, and my learning—technical and people skills—

was not bad. In fact, it was good. I went from a being a developer to leading a team and then directly working with client. I was damn comfortable with my area of responsibility.

I could sit the whole day doing nothing and work for the last two hours and still solve all the pending work. I knew how to solve any damn problem. When *business* came up with a requirement, I could tell which part of the program to change, even without looking at the code. I could solve any production issue within a few minutes.

I continued, because I was in my comfort zone. My ego went up, and then I hit the dreaded stagnation. That's when it started to stink. Eventually, I realized that it was bad for my career. I did not have growth prospects in terms of a higher role, or scope for learning in-demand skills that can help with new job offers.

And you know what the solution is?

It starts with C and ends with E and you just need to HANG in between them. I am talking about CHANGE. I'll be the first to say that change is hard. In fact, change HURTS. But better to hurt rather than stink because of stagnation.

The adaptability to change is a key skill in today's fast-paced environment.

The change journey scares us. How about exploring the whole journey of going from being stagnant to being joyful? Is being joyful good? You bet.

Change manifests into entering a new environment, often in the form of new assignments. A new assignment could be an offer in a new company or a project with a new client within the same company.

Although we might enter with excitement about what we can learn, or do, we quickly realize how much hard work is there ahead of us.

Our initial impressions of the work environment contain an element of fear because we are ignorant of the power relationships between people, the psychology of our boss, the unwritten rules and procedures that are necessary to thrive.

We might get confused—the knowledge needed might go over our heads. We might give in to the feelings of fear, impatience, and confusion. If you give in to these emotions, you will stop observing and learning.

But that's where you need to keep a little patience and courage.

I have personally taken this step and there are only rewards. If you don't give up, and you do allow some time, something remarkable begins to take shape. As we continue to observe and follow the lead of others, we gain clarity, learn the unwritten rules, see how things work that fit together.

If we keep practicing, we gain fluency; basic skills are mastered, allowing us to take on newer and more exciting challenges. We begin to connect things that were invisible to us before. We slowly gain confidence in our ability to solve problems or overcome weaknesses.

We then try out our own ideas. Instead of just learning how others do things, we bring our own flavor into play. Without us knowing, we'll move from a newbie to SME (subject matter expert). And that's when we feel the JOY of doing work.

Now, we are confident to thrive even in a new environment. And this all started because we were ready to CHANGE.

The only thing that matters at work

In 1984, Apple launched the new Macintosh, which was directly handled by Steve Jobs. But, it did not become a hit in the marketplace.

Jobs could not perform to the market's expectations. Jobs wanted Apple executives to focus on Macintosh, instead of the stable Apple II. The board of directors, including then-CEO John Scully, did not agree.

Some say Jobs became a head with no executive powers and so he quit. Some say Jobs was fired. It does not matter how he left Apple. The thing is: he had to leave Apple, the very company he had co-founded.

Fast-forward to 1996; Apple was reeling with poor performance. Gil Amelio, the CEO, had to make things happen to keep up with a competitor like Microsoft which successfully launched Windows 95. Amelio had one solution. He could acquire a company that had all the features that Apple needed. And that's exactly what he did. He acquired a company called NEXT in a multimillion-dollar deal.[3] And guess who was heading NEXT?

That's right. It was Jobs. Jobs returned to Apple as an adviser, then interim CEO, and then the permanent CEO. And then the rest is history.

Can you see the power of performance? Jobs was chucked out because he did not perform. He was later brought back as an adviser after being paid millions of dollars. Why? He performed and built a successful company like NEXT.

The only thing that matters is your *performance*. That's it. Not just in the technology world, but also in areas such as politics, it's performance that matters.

Why did a superpower like the USA reverse its visa ban for Narendra Modi? He was banned from visiting the USA because of his connection to the Gujarat riots.[4] But when Modi became the prime minister of India, all the reasons for the ban went away.

Performance has the power to convince people and get them to see things your way. Some people do politicking and get things done, but it can go only to a certain extent. Performance is a better route because at least you'll feel proud about yourself and your work.

If you are treated like a king, don't get carried away. It's only because you are performing.

There is no secret formula. You just need to perform better than others. You don't need connections. You don't need recommendations. In fact, you build connections and get recommendations through your performance.

If you can perform, eventually you'll get rewarded. If not now, somewhere, somehow, you'll get a reward. Trust me on this.

KEY TAKEAWAYS

- You are in the sales business, not in the software business. Treat every person as a client, whether it is your boss, colleague, or subordinate.

- You are hired for problem solving, not for programming. Our primary job is to solve problems by using programming and other related skills.

- You are an owner, not just an employee. Only by taking ownership of your work will you perform and feel job satisfaction.

- Failure is not an option. Make no mistakes. Your mistakes are often punished and penalized.

- Honesty is not always the best policy. Integrity is the best policy.

- Ego is your enemy. Never develop ego at the workplace. It's just not worth it. However, keep developing rapport with everyone. You never know how it will help you later.

- Sticking longer with a company is not loyalty anymore. Value-add is the new loyalty.

- Perception matters. Learn to see yourself as others see you.

- Comfort zone is a bad place. Change hurts but stagnation stinks. Learn the skill of thriving in new work environments.

- Performance is the only thing that matters at work. Performance does not have a past or future; it is the present. You build connections through performance.

CHAPTER 2

HOW TO DEAL WITH PEOPLE AND POLITICS

In which, we'll learn: strategies to handle the boss, a simple framework for customers, cardinal rules for dealing with colleagues, ideas for a happy relationship with subordinates, politics from Ben Franklin's perspective, and much more

Our performance depends on how well we accustom ourselves to our environment. It is almost impossible to perform if your environment does not support you. That's why it is crucial to get things right with your environment.

Though the word "environment" in the literal sense might seem to mean your cubicle space, or the interior design of the office floor, or the laptop that you are using, the surprising truth is that our environment simply boils down to who we see and what we experience with them.

We techies see people. They could be the boss and related superiors, colleagues, subordinates, or customers. Our experience comes from dealing with these people, and it is this dealing that makes or breaks our performance.

This chapter will focus on dealing with our boss, colleagues, subordinates, and customers. And finally, we will touch the touchy subject of politics.

Boss

You might think your boss is your best buddy—or your worst enemy. I hate to tell you, believe me or not, your boss is your first customer. Treat your boss as a customer. No more, no less.

What is the #1 thing that we should aim to build with our customer? We should strive to build rapport—liking and trust. Even if you forget everything in this book, which I hope not, remember to build rapport with your boss and other people. You'll do really well.

In the current complicated work environment, most of the time, your boss might not be directly overseeing your work. You might be feeling that you are killing it, but your boss might not. That's why it is really important to keep your boss educated about your performance.

Make sure that the person whom you are treating as your boss has direct decision-making authority about your performance and pay hike. This makes it sound like your boss is an owner, which is also true. And that's the beauty of this relationship. Your boss is your customer/owner. The boss needs to buy your work and yet has the responsibility for the work you do.

There is a common thought that people do not perform because of a bad boss. Yes, there are stupid, lunatic, and idiotic bosses. But that's usually an exception. Do you feel that this is not an exception but a norm at your workplace? Then, this should be a strong reason that you need to look for another job. Usually, if people are in the position of a boss, they did something good to reach that level. That's why our lack of performance is not the responsibility of our boss.

It's always our responsibility

Generally, your boss is busy. Your boss will not go the extra mile and suggest the steps you need to take for a good performance rating.

And that's why you need to ASK. I confess that even I hesitated to have this uncomfortable conversation. *But this is one of the simplest steps you can do right now.*

Just have a frank one-on-one conversation about their needs. Get as specific as possible; that'll help you to understand what it takes to achieve your intended performance ratings.

If there are peers working with you, they are your benchmark. Always make sure you are a few steps ahead of them. A little extra that can differentiate you. If you and your peers are doing the same thing, it will be hard for your boss to justify your performance.

In certain cases, you might not report to your boss on a day-to-day basis. You might report to your line manager who is someone between you and your boss. Without overlooking your line manager, establish direct rapport with your true boss whenever you get a chance.

That's because your true boss is the one who will call the final shots. And it's your responsibility to build the rapport with all the relevant bosses.

Go with solutions, not problems

A few years ago, when I was managing a team of 20 folks, a lot of quality issues surfaced. When I questioned my team, it seemed that there was a lack of coordination, which was due to folks not being available during work hours because they were coming in late or not sticking to internal review guidelines.

Things were getting over my head. I felt this was a big risk to the project. I went to my boss and said, "Things are not working well. Folks are not coming on time. Reviews are not happening. If we go on like this, we might not be able to meet our client commitments."

I was expecting, "Good. Thanks for raising the alarm." Instead my boss said, "You came with the problem. What is the solution?"

Ouch. I wanted to say, "You should give me the solution." It was then that I realized that my boss was not a teacher to give answers. He was expecting me to suggest solutions along with the problems.

We need to go with solutions, not just with problems.

Make your boss look good

At the end of the day, having a friendly relationship with your boss helps. But be careful when you are outperforming your boss. Sometimes, bosses get insecure. If the boss is genuine, he or she will let your work get recognized. If the boss is insecure, he or she will not showcase your performance.

You might have heard the phrase, "Your boss is always right." And the reality is that the boss is not always right. But here's the thing: Never make the boss feel that he or she is wrong. That's why it is better to disguise a difference of opinion. Say that a new approach (which you badly want to take) is good for the business, good for the team, or good for the project.

Make the boss feel that if the new ideas are implemented, it will make your boss look good. It's OK for the boss to take credit as long you hold the key.

Another key strategy is to always *align* with your boss on decisions that might be a risk to the project or people. It helps you in two ways. One: your ideas are used to solve the problem. Two: you are making your boss responsible for the decision (just in case you face glitches).

Just keep one last thing in mind: Always introduce ideas or suggestions by stating how it will benefit the other person, not how will it benefit you. This is a great persuasion technique—even with colleagues, clients, friends and family—to sell your ideas.

Agree to disagree with your boss

You'll always have aspirations when you work. And these will keep changing at different experience levels. Conversation topics could be work-from-home, working at a client location, moving to a different project, following a specific process, salary raise, promotion, or any other topic that can create disagreements. Your boss will usually give an explanation that supports the organization when turning you down.

You might find the explanation ridiculous. Deep down, even your boss might know that it is nonsense. And when you face it, please do not take it personally. It's the boss's role that might be prompting such explanations. You might ask, why have such uncomfortable conversations when you know that nothing is going to happen about it?

Look, all aspirations will not be met. But only if you ask, and only if it floats around, somewhere, someone will hear about it and something good might come out of it.

But, if you take it personally, get demotivated and speak in a rash way, everything will go out the window. Hence, agree to disagree with your boss. Always maintain a good rapport with your boss and stakeholders. That's what matters.

Be genuinely helpful

You might be a rock star at what you do but if what you are doing is not helping your boss, chances are that your work won't matter. That's why we need to understand the motivations and expectations of our boss. Your boss is not the ultimate boss. Even the boss has a boss, who has a boss.

Figure out what your boss wants and be genuinely helpful. If your boss wants help in creating a client proposal, do it. If your boss needs help with creating a presentation, do it. But take care that you don't lose focus on your core work. All the help you provide must be in addition to your core competence.

What if you have a boss who is not sensible? Well, that's what we will cover next.

How to deal with a micromanager

Good bosses will not micromanage. Instead, a good boss will give you autonomy, which is one of the three drivers that motivate employees.

Daniel H. Pink talks about this in his bestselling book *Drive*. The three things that motivate employees are autonomy, purpose, and mastery. And if a bad boss tries to take the autonomy away—by micromanaging or behaving like a lunatic—from a good employee, it leads to poor performance.

It's a human tendency to micromanage. Sometimes, even I do it. It's painful for me as well. People have different reasons. But, the most common reason for micromanagement is *lack of trust*.

If you know that your boss is not micromanaging others and just you, then you must build trust. Be patient and stick to your guns in delivering work. Once you build the trust, trust me that your boss will leave you alone.

If things are getting stalled and maybe the lack of freedom is impacting your performance, talk to your boss about the situation. Make it clear that it is hurting your performance. Most bosses will leave you alone because you took the initiative to talk and resolve the issue—which shows your maturity.

Still, there are suckers who might not get it. And that's why you need to know the micro-reporter technique. You become a *micro reporter.* You become extremely welcoming. You involve your micromanaging boss in every single piece of work that is possible. You include the boss in emails, meeting invites, minutes of meetings, and every discussion. Before the micromanager can ask your status, you update the status.

Before the micromanager asks you why the problem is not solved, you give an update on all the possible steps you took to solve the problem. In addition, you ask the micromanager to help you in solving the problem.

Before the micromanager asks why you are not logged in early in the morning, you send a note that you'll be late with reasons such as personal emergency, or stayed late the previous day.

Before the micromanager follows up on why you could not work on task B, you say that you are not able to work on task B because task A is taking all your time. Ask if you should stop work on task A in order to start task B.

Before the micromanager asks you to explain a delay in progress on the project, you detail the issues: other team members are not available to solve problems, the right stakeholders are not available to answer questions, the business partner is a hard nut to crack, or any other practical reason.

Did you observe, even here, it boils down to performance? Though being under a micromanager is not so ideal, there is one advantage: You won't have to feel responsible if something goes wrong. You can say that the micromanager was always updated.

How to deal with a lunatic boss

In your life outside of work, you won't find lunatics most of the time, but you might find a few along the way. Similarly, you might encounter a few lunatics along the way in your work career.

They are just that: lunatics. You'll wonder how on earth they got there. God knows. They impersonated some other person. They bribed HR into hiring them, they had the right relatives, or they slept with the right person. It might be a good idea if you stop finding reasons, and start understanding their motivations.

Sometimes, it could be the situation that is driving your boss to behave like a lunatic. Assess the situation. If you are really working for a critical project that has very high visibility, then you can stretch yourself. But that has to be an exception, not a norm.

Your boss can be called a long-term lunatic if you are *always* asked to log in sharp at 9 a.m. and work till you burn the midnight oil, or *always* work on impossible schedules. Some might say that you need to fight out such toxic bosses.

Honestly, it is not worth fighting. It's a losing battle. Hence, move out of the assignment when you are sure that your boss is a long-term lunatic. If you are bound to stay because of other constraints, then be ready to *escalate* the situation. Again, do this only if you trust your line of management. Otherwise it's just not worth it. If the whole line of management is behaving like lunatics—then you can't do much.

Customers

Customer is God is a Japanese proverb, which has been made famous by technology stalwarts. But, we don't need to learn customer value from Bill Gates, Mark Zuckerberg, Narayana Murthy, or Jeff Bezos.

We can learn it from Anna Durai, an auto-rickshaw driver who runs his auto in the Old Mahabalipuram Road, otherwise known as the IT corridor of Chennai, India. There is a reason why I use his example. He is from a humble background, does not have a regular education, does not know English, does not work in a sophisticated environment like the techies, and must fight with the not-so-sophisticated traffic system—unlike the one in the USA—in India.

Yet he has given multiple TEDx talks about customer value![1] He does not even drive a cab for a sophisticated tech company like Uber. He drives a share-auto rickshaw.

Share-auto rickshaw is an innovative transport mechanism, which is a different story altogether. It has a minimum of six seats, and it might not be an exaggeration if I say that share-auto is one of the transport lifelines in India, connecting people to places where public transport is insufficient or unavailable.

But where Anna Durai has hit a home run is how he serves his customers, even though he only drives a share auto. He provides his passengers with all the current newspapers and latest magazines, tablet, laptop, Wi-Fi, swiping machine for card payment, and heck more within his auto-rickshaw!

When I saw his work, and heard his talk about customer value, I was humbled. I am translating his words into English. He said, "You all are working for very big companies. You all know a lot of things. If I can do so many things for my customers, I am sure you can do many more things for your customers."

He is referring to client delight, which has been the go-to mantra for the tech companies. This is obvious. But what is not obvious—which took a lot of years to dawn on me—is:

We need to give solutions, not just take orders.

Order taking is doing as told. A receptionist at a hotel is an order taker. I don't demean the receptionist's job. They too solve problems when hotel booking is messed up. However, their default mode is taking orders. But our default mode should be giving solutions.

I used to think that I was doing well by doing what my clients were asking me to do. But, that is not how we can differentiate ourselves.

Our clients are busy most of the time. That's how companies are designed. We can't help it. Everyone is trying to get stuff done with the least possible overhead.

We should find out—by researching or asking or observing them during meetings—the needs of our clients, and then give solutions. Remember that I argued that we are problem solvers rather than programmers. And problem solvers *give solutions to our clients*. To do so:

1. Recognize the customer

Based on whether you work in software service or product, the customer avatar might change. As techies working for business applications, we usually serve our business partners, along with other program management partners. As techies working for a software product, we serve our customers, either a direct consumer or another company.

You might be accountable for multiple customers. If that's the case, you need to satisfy the problems of all the stakeholders. Sometimes you might not have client interaction. But identify who will benefit from the work you are doing. If you are not sure, ask people around on who is your stakeholder.

2. See every task as a problem

By and large, you'll be solving two kinds of problems. One is a proactive problem, and the other one is a reactive problem.

Proactive problems are related to requirements, design, and development. These represent the high-level stages of a software development lifecycle, but every stage is a proactive problem of its own.

Reactive problems are related to operations where the functioning software fails. This could be a report not generated on time, a job that did not complete, a web page not responding for peak traffic, or any other issue where you'll need to debug and come up with solutions. They are challenging yet enriching because you need to solve issues under tight timelines.

We can very well consider the above problems as tasks but at the heart of any task, we are trying to solve a problem, a need of our customers. So it is essential that we learn to see every task as a problem statement and find an answer.

3. Solve the problem

Our first priority is to solve the customer's problem. That's how we are going to build rapport with our clients. When a problem arises, whether technical or business, understanding the big picture and narrowing down the scope of the issue is what matters. And for that you need to ask questions that make sense.

For proactive problems, ask:

- What does the customer want?

- By when does the customer want it? Are the dates fixed? If dates are fixed, can the scope be flexible?

- Can a tactical solution (short term) be better? Or will a strategic solution (long term) be better?

- Does the customer even know about non-functional requirements (NFRs) such as performance or load capacity, stress test, or any other NFR?

For reactive problems, ask:

- Why did the process fail? Did it fail because our application logic was incorrect? Or because the input data was not as per the expectation?

- Or did it fail because the number of system users increased?

- How can we fix it so that it doesn't repeat?

I have come to understand that it is not necessary that I alone bear the brunt of any problem. Nobody is conducting an exam where we should focus only on our computer without looking here and there. And we won't be expelled when we ask for help. Unlike school or college, we'll be appreciated when we solve problems, whether we reuse an existing piece of code or use someone else's help.

At the end of the day, the solution is what matters. However, when we offer solutions, we need to give all relevant options, along with the pros and cons of each option, and then highlight the recommended option.

In today's current chaotic software systems, you'll be able to give proper solutions only if you have the business knowledge that the software is built for. Whether it is a software application for B2B (business to business) or B2C (business to consumers), knowing and understanding the business side of the software helps immensely in solving problems.

What I have covered here is the core of how we need to handle customers. We need to have customer obsession to win in the marketplace. And you and I are the soldiers who work at the ground level for our companies to win in the marketplace.

I'll talk more about dealing with customers in the chapter related to speaking, where I'll cover how to speak with our clients.

Colleagues

During my college days, most of the folks used to call me an extrovert. Now, people at my work call me an introvert. And I am like, "this is interesting." Probably, the change from an extrovert to an introvert is natural, as we grow older.

Extrovert and introvert are states at the extreme ends of a scale. And we fluctuate somewhere between those states, based on people—colleagues, friends, relatives—and situations such as no pressure, high pressure, or a friendly atmosphere.

The problem is that we become an extrovert when we are supposed to act like an introvert, and become an introvert when we are supposed to act like an extrovert.

Your performance is not just an individual measure; it is also a function of how you deal with your colleagues. Teamwork is important and we always need to think WIN-WIN situations. I think we all understand this and there is enough said about this concept.

What I'll cover here are four cardinal rules that will guide you in dealing with colleagues.

Cardinal Rule #1

You need to be careful in making sure that your superior (boss or client) knows your contribution (whole or partial) to the delivered work.

You'll find different kinds of colleagues, and among them all, you need to watch out for opportunists. Opportunists are folks just waiting for opportunities to seamlessly associate themselves with any good work.

If you are not careful, the credit for your hard work could be shared, which happens most of the time. Be very careful. This is especially true with bigger teams.

Cardinal Rule #2

Never try to change colleagues who don't want to change.

In a work culture, especially in bigger teams, there will be certain unwritten rules. For example, following a particular process (even outdated), clubbing after office hours, gossiping about stuff, or any unwritten cultural rules. You could love or hate them.

Group dynamics are very interesting. The moment you try to suggest something different, thinking of the larger good, people will resist it. They'll do all in their power not to change it. They'll see as you as a threat. They might even backbite you.

The smart thing is to not share your opinions in a direct way. However, you can subtly talk them into ideas that seem as if they are the group's idea. Again, this is a skill you need to learn. Never try to rebel or to change other people's rigid ideas. It's just not worth your time.

Wait for the right opportunity or save your ideas for your own company (whenever you start one). Just don't impose your ideas on others.

The legendary German poet Goethe said, "It is a great folly to hope that other men will harmonize with us; I have never hoped this. I have always regarded each man as an independent individual, whom I endeavored to understand with all his peculiarities, but from whom I desired no further sympathy. In this way have I been enabled to converse with every man, and thus alone is produced the knowledge of various characters and the dexterity necessary for the conduct of life."

Cardinal Rule #3

Don't get into the habit of helping others when your work is pending. Always finish your work first, before helping others.

Rahul is a techie working for a few years in a multinational software services company. He learns things quickly, can communicate well, and shows the spirit of doing things. Whenever his colleague has a problem, Rahul solves the problem pretty quickly. Rahul is killing it.

Then one day, his superior takes him to a conference room and says, "Rahul, you need to improve your performance." Rahul is taken aback. The superior continues, "You seem to help others and leave your work pending."

And I feel Rahul's superior is right. However, Rahul's superior might have had a different feedback if Rahul had followed rule #3.

I'm not telling that you should not help others when you have pending work. You should help the first time. But, you should avoid helping someone with the same problem in a repeated fashion. One practical way to handle this situation is asking them to document things. When you are giving training, or helping people with a problem, ask them to document it. It could be jotting down the steps in a notepad or saving it as a Word document. Documenting things for later reference will really help people, and yet few people do this.

Cardinal Rule #4

Never get too close, too quickly with your colleagues.

During one of my assignments, I established a good rapport with a colleague. We started talking about things apart from work as well. It was going good and then one day, I went to my colleague's desk.

My colleague was watching something on the phone. Out of curiosity, I peeped in to check it out. And boom came the reply, "Don't you have any manners of not peeping into someone's personal space?"

I was shocked.

Nobody had used such harsh words with me. I just could not react. I said, "I am sorry." And I think those were the last words I ever spoke to that colleague. I am not going to argue about who was right; instead, I am going to expand on this cardinal rule.

I am not saying that you should not build friendships with colleagues. You should and that'll help you in the long run. And for such relationships to form, it takes time. At least till you reach that level, be cautious when commenting on sex, religion, politics, or any other sensitive topics. You never know how it might backfire.

And that's why it is important to maintain your friendship with buddies from high school or college with whom you shared a great rapport. It's good to meet with them, let your hair down, and discuss your thoughts about life. This is more important than we can imagine. We'll see why and how in the section related to emotional needs in Chapter 8.

Subordinates

After a few years in any assignment, we are bound to gain some expertise and we'll be responsible for new techies. Our performance will also depend on how we get productive work out of them.

Now we are talking about skills that'll be needed to perform as a boss. Here's the thing. If people are really good at what they are doing, leave them alone. Seriously, just because you must oversee their work or are supposed to keep track of them, don't nag them.

It doesn't matter if you have the title of manager or a lead or whatever, leave the good ones alone. For some slow learners, if you trust them and instill a sense of ownership, people deliver.

Having said that, we should not forget to follow up and follow through on their work. We need to keep track of their work, but our subordinates should not get a feeling that we are micromanaging them.

You'll find non-performing subordinates as well. Here's what I do to handle them. If they show interest to learn, but they are slow to catch up, I'll give them some extra support. If they are not willing to learn, I'll let them go from my team at the first chance.

The following three simple rules will go a long way in achieving performance with your subordinates.

Give time and instill trust

Your subordinates need time to tune into the work, especially if it's a new type of task that they are doing. Do not blame them if they are not able to handle situations. As a superior, you need to support them when they are stuck.

Trust them and find opportunities to encourage them. Say, "I'm sure you can do it." When they do the work quickly or on their own, a simple and genuine appreciation of "Good work" will make their day. People, including you or me, love appreciations. Allow them to get their hands dirty while they are learning. It's okay to show tough love but you should not make them feel that they are useless.

Yes, sometimes it will test our patience, and that's why it's a good idea to have a buffer—add 10 or 20 percent more time—to the ETA of the subordinate's task.

Trust me, people deliver in response to the trust that you show them. Personally, my performance increases like crazy when my client or boss trusts me and does not meddle with my work.

Make them accountable

Though you are good with your subordinates, you should not lose track of their work. We'll see more about follow-through and follow-up in the next chapter, but the easiest and most effective way to track the work of your subordinates is to make them accountable.

For example, instead of you giving a time frame to complete a task, ask them, "Can you please advise me by when I can expect a reply?"

If you are responsible for many subordinates, then one simple technique which worked really well for me was to create a table with the following headings: Serial number, Project or High-level task name, Detailed task, Assignee name, ETA.

Every morning, I filled in the details and sent it to the team. Yes, it takes some time but creating this and sending it to the entire team was worth the effort. Everyone knew what everyone else was doing. That established transparency, which in turn established accountability. From a long-term perspective, it provided traceability. Anyone can track who worked on which task, when they worked, and how much work each subordinate did for a specific time period.

Lead, not manage

You don't need a title to do the role of a lead.

A manager will only take status reports. A leader will not only take status updates but also give a helping hand when things are not going according to the plan.

A manager will not take the responsibility for a production defect. A leader will take collective responsibility for the team and definitely not point out the mistake of an individual.

People by default are inclined to follow because that's how we are wired. People don't follow managers; people follow leaders.

The moment you play the role of a lead, you give your subordinates a solid reason why they should work for you. And that will inspire them to work for you with blood and sweat.

Until now, we discussed how to deal with people. Now, let's see how to handle the politics.

Office politics

All our childhood, we are surrounded by authoritative and/or loving figures. We idolize our parents and teachers. We trust whatever they say. We feel emotionally obliged to do what they do or say.

Once we complete our education and enter the "real" world, we end up searching for a father figure in a boss, or a college buddy in a colleague. We don't realize that everyone is there thinking "what's in it for me."

People are just trying to survive. If we don't see them as normal people, with the same set of insecurities as we have, we'll fail to recognize their true intentions.

And true intention is the root cause of politics.

Office politics is something that most people do not like to talk about or get involved with. It's not something that happens in front of you. It's something that happens around you.

People who are involved with office politics are like bad drivers on the road. You ignore them and you'll be in trouble. The only way is to be careful and navigate your way.

Pericles, a statesman in ancient Greece, rightly said, "Just because you do not take an interest in politics doesn't mean politics won't take an interest in you." This is true even today.

Don't worry if you are facing politics and don't be happy if you are not. You'll be at a loss if you don't face it because you have missed a chance to learn this invaluable skill. In today's cutthroat competitive environments, you need to at least have basic awareness to navigate these barriers.

Handling office politics boils down to the ability to see people's true intentions and act accordingly.

I came across Benjamin Franklin's story while reading Robert Greene's *Mastery.* It's a perfect example to understand how true intentions work and what to do about it.

Franklin was a multifaceted, multi-skilled personality. He was one of America's founders, a publisher, author, scientist, inventor, and more importantly, a successful politician. I don't know how he managed success in all these roles. Probably, that's why he is still remembered!

Ben was born to a poor family. One among many siblings, he dropped out of school because of lack of money, but he had a flair for reading and writing. His brother James had a flair for publishing, and Ben also learned the publishing trade.

When Ben was 15, James started the *New England Courant,* a newspaper business. Ben was excited and wanted to write for the paper but James would not let him. But Ben was determined, so he wrote to the newspaper as an outsider under the pseudonym of Silence Dogood. The articles became a big hit. Unable to hide it anymore, Ben confessed to James about Silence Dogood.

To Ben's surprise, James became furious. Their differences grew and Ben ran away to Philadelphia and started working in a printing business under Samuel Keimer.

One day, Ben met the governor of the colony of Pennsylvania, William Keith. The governor was impressed with Ben. Keith said he would help Ben to set up a printing business and provide the initial amount to start the shop. The machines and material had to come from London, so Keith asked Ben to go to London to supervise the acquisition.

After a few months, no money came from Keith, but the governor's office wrote back that letters of credit would be waiting as soon as Ben landed in London.

Ben quit his job without informing Samuel, his current employer, and booked his voyage to London. But when Ben landed in London, nobody was waiting. Ben could not believe this. He searched for government representatives and an American merchant told Ben that Keith was a man of empty promises.

Ben was shaken but he was not completely at a loss. London was a great place for Ben's skillsets in printing. He found a job. He showed his talent for printing and publishing. But, he soon faced another hurdle. His co-workers drank beer during the day and everyone was expected to contribute to the beer fund. Ben did not like the idea of drinking during work hours. So, he did not agree to contribute his hard-earned money.

He soon realized that something wrong was happening. Even after he proofread, there were mistakes being found in articles. The quality of his work was going down. Ben realized that if he did not control this, he might get fired.

When Ben discussed the quality issues with some of his co-workers, he was told that a ghost came after the people who did not contribute to the beer fund. When Ben contributed to the fund, apparently the quality issues also vanished.

After all this, Ben realized something important:

Being naive is not good.

He realized that James became furious not because Ben cheated, but because James was jealous of Ben.

Ben realized that it was his mistake to trust the governor naively. He should have realized that the governor was full of false promises when the governor did not give him the promised money.

Ben realized that being self-righteous at work does not help. He had almost paid the price for going away from the culture.

So, he decided he would not trust what anyone said. He would not get emotional but remain detached. He would always try to see people's true intentions.

And this decision helped him when he went back to Philadelphia. When Ben was looking for work back in Philadelphia, he met his earlier employer Samuel. Though Ben had quit without notice, Samuel offered him a nice position. Ben would be in charge of the staff and train a few others to run Samuel's other shops.

But Ben felt something was not right. Samuel agreed to a nice yearly salary and appeared more friendly than usual. Ben, who had learned his lessons in life, took a step back and assessed the situation. Samuel should have been furious with Ben because he left the job without notice. Now, he was asking Ben to train others.

Ben thought about it. And he was right. Samuel had other plans. Once Ben trained the others, Samuel was planning to fire Ben. Ben understood Samuel's true intention.

Instead of succumbing to Samuel's plan, he changed the circumstances to his favor. Ben used his managerial position to build connections with merchants and customers. When Samuel was out, he learned new skills in the printing business.

When Ben felt Samuel was going to make his move, Ben quit and set up his own shop. He was ready with financial backing, greater publishing knowledge, and a set of customers who would follow him anywhere.

By understanding Samuel's true intentions, Ben did not feel guilty about his move. In fact, Ben felt that he was playing a game of chess, and that's what it is all about.

It's a game.

Stop trusting and believing what anyone says and does. What you hear is not what is true. That does not mean you don't act upon what someone says. What I am saying is don't do work naively without knowing the true intent.

If your boss offers you a promotion in the coming cycle to stop you from quitting and clearly your department does not seem to be growing, then you need to take a step back and think again about the intention.

If your co-workers are very friendly to you but backbiting about other co-workers, you need to take a step back and think about the intention. Are you sure that they'll not backbite against you to someone else?

If your boss is saying that you'll get a good performance rating, but you don't have any awards, recognition, or client appreciation, then chances are that it's a bluff with you to get past the next few months.

Apart from learning to recognize the true intentions of folks at work, remember the steps below to proactively navigate office politics.

Build key connections

Apart from corporate hierarchy, try to build connections and rapport with your unit head, or the boss of your boss. It does not mean that you'll use this to game the system, but building key connections at the top level will help if some problem surfaces tomorrow. You'll at least have a fair chance to make a strong case.

Be neutral with "bad" politicians

To put it simply, "bad" politicians are the ones who somehow got into the company. They don't have any intention to work hard or grow through performance. It will be stupid of you to try to change them. And it will be stupid of you to refrain from dealing with them. As long as you are polite and professional with these folks, you are good.

Now that we have taken a dive into people and politics, in the next chapter we'll see the core performance mechanics—how to get more with less.

KEY TAKEAWAYS

- Treat your boss as a customer. Our performance is our responsibility. Go to your boss with solutions, not just with problems. Make your boss look good. Agree to disagree and move on. Be genuinely helpful to your boss.

- Customer is God. We need to give solutions to our clients' problems, not just take orders. Build rapport with your clients by solving their problems.

- Always strive to create WIN-WIN situations when dealing with colleagues. Make sure that your superior knows your contribution. Never try to change colleagues who don't want to change. Don't get into the habit of helping others before clearing your plate. Never get too close, too quickly with your colleagues.

- Give sufficient time and build trust with your subordinates. Leave the good ones alone, and let go the bad ones. Make them accountable, but don't forget to follow up or follow through. Lead them by supporting, not micromanaging them.

- Handling office politics boils down to understanding people's true intention and acting accordingly. Apart from that, building key connections with your line of management and being neutral with bad politicians will help greatly.

CHAPTER 3

HOW TO GET MORE
DONE WITH LESS

In which, we'll learn: Parkinson's law, when and when not to multitask, Eisenhower's priority matrix for techies, active time, 80/20 rule, how to use follow-up and follow-through, value versus process, and how to use manual and digital note taking to do more

When I was working at my employer's base location, I used to work from 10 in the morning till seven in the evening. When I was working at the client location, I would start work at nine in the morning, finish 90 percent of my work by five in the evening and complete the remaining 10 percent by logging in for a few hours at night.

The amount of work I completed while working in the client location was like two to three times the work I did while working at my base location. It was then I realized how unproductive I used to be earlier. Again, the environment at the client location made the difference. I had access to client resources, which was not the case while working at my base location. What I am trying to point out is that *work expands with the available time.*

This was not some discovery of mine. It was first observed and articulated by Cyril Northcote Parkinson in 1955. He published *Parkinson's Law* in 1958. In this book, he says, "work expands so as to fill the time available for its completion," which is also known as Parkinson's Law.[1] The law describes that a task will continue to swell in importance and complexity according to the time allotted to complete the task.

Work becomes like the universe, and it keeps expanding and expanding to fit the time. We end up doing less with more, whereas what we want is *more with less*.

Talking about more, there is no better word than "multitasking," which is what we will address now.

Multitasking

Multitasking seems to be one of the greatest innovations in the information technology revolution. Yet multitasking has a bad rap. Check out the facts from a leading publication:[2]

- They (*multitaskers*) were up to 40 percent slower.

- After 20 minutes of interrupted performance, people report significantly higher stress levels, frustration, workload, effort, and pressure.

- Multitasking is a significant reason why we are witnessing epidemics of rage, believes Dr. Alan Keen, a behavioral scientist.

Why has multitasking become all the rage?

Let me share a short story. As a techie, you might know this. Long, long ago, maybe not so long ago, there was the single processor computer. It did a good job of performing one task at a time. But people hated to see tasks waiting. So, multiprocessor computers were invented. Now, the computer could finish multiple tasks in parallel. That was awesome, but the story did not end there.

People felt that if a computer can multitask, why can't a techie? So, work was assigned to a techie in a parallel manner. The techie started doing multiple projects while talking on multiple channels such as instant message, cell phone, or desk phone. But just think about it. No one—not just a techie—can truly multitask. You cannot give 100 percent attention to task A and 100 percent attention to task B.

What we are doing is either dividing attention among multiple things or juggling between task A and task B in a hyperactive fashion, and in the process not giving quality attention to any task.

I don't think we need scientific research to prove this. If you have been working for a while, you know what I am talking about. But, we also know that a demanding work environment forces us to handle multiple things.

And honestly, we cannot ignore multitasking.

Apart from our core work, we have to respond to emails while being on a call, keep asking for updates, raise issues, talk to multiple stakeholders, wear multiple hats in the absence of colleagues, and a zillion other things that come our way. And we certainly cannot go into a silo and say that I read an article in BBC that says my IQ will drop by 10 percent if I juggle too much information.[3] Your boss will say, "Then, I don't need you."

Instead of saying, "I won't multitask," ask, "How do we manage multitasking situations?"

Largely, there are two types of work: creative and non-creative.

Non-creative is where you need to apply a set of rules or steps and you get the solution. For example, creating a sales report, running queries, following up with someone, attending regular status calls, or replying to emails. It's not complicated. You follow the steps and boom—you get through this stuff.

The creative work is where you cannot apply a set of steps to arrive at the solution. It involves tasks related to design, algorithms, logic, unknown production issues, replying to critical emails, attending critical meetings, or any activity that needs more focus and attention. These are more difficult problems to solve. I could have used critical work as a general term, but I used creative because when pushed to get things done, you need to be creative.

The rule of thumb is to *do light multitasking during non-creative work and NO multitasking during creative work.*

Light multitasking means sending a quick one-word or one-sentence reply to a time-sensitive email or quickly giving your status updates in a meeting and exiting. If pressed to stay in the meeting, you then say, "Please give me a shout if you need me. I'll be available on call but will be passive."

Ok, I said not to multitask for creative work. So, what should we do? We'll use the power of *uninterrupted work.*

Before that, let me tell you what happened with Alan. Alan was working on a design. He sat for an hour and figured out that there were eight different elements that impacted his design. He was about to crack the design when he heard a "ping." He checked his instant messenger. Sweetie from the adjacent cubicle had sent him a smiley. And Alan's face glowed like a 100-watt bulb. By the time Alan finished his sweet exchange of messages, he had lost the approach to create the design. A story with a similar ending is happening in every cubicle.

While doing creative work, you cannot keep getting interrupted because you cannot resume exactly where you left off. It's going to take some time before your brain goes into that zone. It's like REM sleep where you'll need to spend some time in bed before the REM sleep kicks. If someone disturbs you in between, you have to start again. It's the same while you try to do creative work.

You need at least two to four hours of uninterrupted time to do critical work. It's the "me" time when you'll finish work that really matters. And this needs full focus. Be careful not to be tempted to answer a simple email or an instant message. You might not have realized this but there is a switching cost that you incur when you move from one task to another. It is like an additional IO that happened.

From a movie standpoint, if productivity is the hero, then interruption is the villain. Hence, turn off all bells and whistles. If turning instant messenger status to *do-not-disturb* mode helps, then do it. If working from a conference room helps, then do it. If keeping your cell phone on silent mode helps, then do it.

Do whatever it takes it to protect and produce good quality work.

Priority should be priority

When you start work, there will be hundreds of distractions. You might be getting instant messages for work, for gossip, or whatever. Your cubicle mate might call you to have coffee or chitchat. Your eyes might fall on your Facebook page, or you might start getting messages on your smartphone.

A hundred things can happen. On top of this, if you successfully open your inbox and sift through emails, you figure out that there are 10 things that need your attention. Where do you start, and how do you handle this?

That's why *priority* is so important. And to determine what takes priority, let us leverage the Eisenhower decision matrix, the model used by Dwight D. Eisenhower to be a successful general and president. Though it sounds theoretical, once you use it, it will become second nature to you. This is what it is:

Imagine four quadrants and classify each task: Q1 (important and urgent), Q2 (important but not urgent), Q3 (not important, but urgent), Q4 (not important, not urgent). What the model recommends is to prioritize tasks based on the following order: Q1, Q2, Q3, Q4.

Since we are talking about urgent and important tasks, let us define them as well.

Urgent means that a task requires immediate attention. These are the to-dos that shout "Now!" Urgent tasks put us in a *reactive* mode; one marked by a defensive, negative, hurried, and narrowly focused mindset.

Important means that it can contribute to our goals, and in turn our performance. When we focus on important activities we operate in a *responsive* mode, which helps us remain calm, and rational.

Sometimes important tasks are also urgent, but typically need not be. It is focusing on important activities that will lead to better performance.

In *The 7 Habits of Highly Effective People,* Stephen Covey discussed the Eisenhower decision matrix from a common person's perspective. Let me cover this from a techie's perspective.

Q1 tasks (important and urgent) could be:

- Production issues: jobs on hold, data issues in file, slow response of software application, or any software functionality that is broken or not working as expected.

- Deadline issues: problems impacting any critical project's delivery, critical resources on leave or infrastructure shutdown, client escalations, or anything that is not delivered on time.

Q2 tasks (important but not urgent) could be:

- Self-learning: understanding technologies of the software application, as well as the business use of the software application.

- Core work: designing, coding, solution discussion, testing, and requirement elicitation.

- Asset creation: creating tools, developing POCs (proof of concepts), macros, reports, documents, or anything that will reduce time or effort.

- Voluntary support: genuinely giving a helping hand to superiors; helping other team members to solve a critical problem (make sure you keep this official so that your superiors know about your contribution).

- Training others: taking sessions and teaching skills to others in your team or to the whole unit. The larger the group, the better the impact.

- Self-care: drinking water, walking once every two hours, sitting in proper posture.

Q3 tasks (not important but urgent) could be:

- Communicating: instant messages, unplanned meetings, official calls on mobile, extension of planned meetings, clarification emails.

- Interrupted support: colleagues walking to your desk for help, interfacing application or team needing support.

Q4 tasks (not important and not urgent) could be:

Anything that does not fall in the above categories shall fall into Q4. All ETAs (estimated time of arrivals) being equal, it is best to attempt

Q4 tasks in the following order: clients, boss, and stakeholders.

We saw when to multitask, and how to prioritize, but we also need to do the right thing at the right time. That's what we'll see next.

All hours are not the same

Have you observed why Mark Zuckerberg, Steve Jobs, and Barack Obama wear similar dress time and again?

During his final stint at Apple, Jobs famously wore the same black turtleneck, blue jeans, and similar sneakers every day. Zuckerberg wears his grey T-shirt. "I really want to clear my life to make it so that I have to make as few decisions as possible about anything except how to best serve this community," said Zuckerberg during an online Q&A session.[4]

As Obama told *Vanity Fair*, "You'll see I wear only gray or blue suits. I'm trying to pare down decisions. I don't want to make decisions about what I'm eating or wearing. Because I have too many other decisions to make."[5]

If you have read between the lines, you will see they are not trying to save time. They are trying to save *active time*, which can be used for doing the most impactful work. I think that's a big takeaway.

And that's why I want you to understand that your active time is finite and you must be careful where and how you use it. That's why all hours in the day are not the same.

We perform at peak levels only during certain hours. Our cylinders fire 100 percent only for some hours in a day, and at different times for different people.

For some, peak performance is usually between 10 a.m. and 1 p.m. For some folks, it could be 2 p.m. to 5 p.m. The hour of the day does not matter.

Just observe what time of the day you perform to the fullest. And remember to protect that peak time for your most important activities, especially the Q1 and Q2 tasks that we discussed in the previous section.

Most of the time, we end up spending more time on Q3 tasks rather than Q2 tasks and the main time-suck is a meeting. Most meetings fall under Q3 (urgent, not important) tasks. First understand whether the meeting is organized to do anything productive, solving real problems, or whether it is just a status-tracking meeting.

If it is a status-tracking meeting, avoid it at all costs. Just send an email update. If they insist, join the call and say, "I need to attend to something else that has come up. Can I quickly give my update?" Usually you'll get a "sure" and then continue saying your update, "I am currently 50 percent done. I'll have a draft of design ready by tomorrow EOD." Then pause for a few seconds before dropping off.

You goal is to work on as many Q1 and Q2 tasks during your peak performance hours and push Q3 and Q4 tasks to the remaining hours. If possible, delegate Q3 and Q4 tasks to others.

Insight from Vilfredo Pareto

In 1896, Vilfredo Pareto, through his first paper *Cours d'économie politique*, published an interesting insight.[6] He stated that 80 percent of the land in Italy was controlled by 20 percent of the men. The Pareto rule (also well known as the 80/20 rule) states that 80 percent of effects come from 20 percent of causes.

- Have you observed that only 20 percent of the people in a team are responsible for 80 percent of the results?

- Have you observed that only 20 percent of your friends support you 80 percent of the time?

- Do you wear only 20 percent of your clothes 80 percent of the time?

The fraction might not be exactly 80/20. However, the essence is true—causes and effects are not directly proportional. This is such a powerful rule that it can be used as a rule of thumb to optimize your time, efforts, and resources.

You can find which 20 percent of tasks are reasons for 80 percent of the results. You can put more effort on that 20 percent.

This principle applies to almost all areas of our life.

Your mom was right when she was telling you to hang out with good guys and gals. Find which 20 percent of people at work or in your life are helping 80 percent of the time. Focus your efforts in helping and serving those 20 percent.

This rule is so powerful that if you start applying it in all areas of life, you can become way more effective—rather than just productive—than your current levels.

Follow up & follow through

There are two common mistakes which techies—or anyone—can make.

- Mistake one: stopping the work when not sure which way to proceed.

- Mistake two: making convenient or stupid assumptions so that the work becomes easy to complete.

If you don't want to be affected by such mistakes, you better learn to follow up and follow through. When you can truly understand and implement these two skills, half of your work will be taken care of.

First, let us understand the difference. Follow-up is the additional nudge on any agreed deadline.

For example, the team handling Application A confirmed that they'd send some sample data after two days. Now after two days, you have not gotten any note from the team. What will you do? You'll obviously ask them.

This is follow-up.

I think many understand follow-up. However, follow-through is something that is often misunderstood and underutilized.

Follow-through is seeing something through to completion. Let us extend the same example to create a new scenario. You need to get data from team A, process the data in a day's time, and send it to team B. The whole activity needs to complete in five days. The team handling Application A confirmed that they'd send sample data after two days. And you are responsible for the activity to be done within five days. Instead of waiting for two days, it would be a good idea to *send a note the day before the delivery was promised*:

> Hi Tom
>
> Hope you are keeping well. Just checking in to make sure that you are all set to send the sample data tomorrow.
>
> Thanks
> Rama

If things are going well, Tom will say, "Yes, we are all set." If Tom does not reply, you get a hint that things are not good. You can now proactively involve the necessary stakeholders (make sure Tom's boss is in the loop) and ask for a response.

Now team A has woken up and sent the data by the middle of the third day. *You immediately check the data and see if there are any is-*

sues with the quality. If you find any quality issues, then respond asking for clarification. You still keep all stakeholders in copy.

You sort out all issues by going back and forth. By the end of the third day, team A gives quality sample data. You process it within 24 hours and send the data back to team B by the end of the fourth day. *You just don't send it, you ask team B to check and confirm that your file does not have any quality issues.* This way, you are sure that things are good from your end.

The activities that represent follow-through are highlighted in italics. If you can learn to follow through properly, you'll get more work to completion in less time.

Till now, we learned the key principles to get more done with less. But there's one thing that is supposed to help, but often hampers. And that is coming next.

Process is not the thing

If interruption is one thing, process is another to dampen your goal of doing more with less. Heck, if not handled well, process won't allow you to do anything at all.

Some time ago, my client assignment came to an end. I was part of the finance unit in my company. While I was attending other client interviews through the finance unit, my profile got mapped to the insurance unit, without any rhyme or reason.

My interview with a finance client got cleared. The project manager from the finance unit was trying to map me in the company portal. He could not proceed because now I was part of the insurance unit. He sent an email on a Friday evening to the talent manager of the insurance unit to release me from the insurance unit.

When I came in on Monday morning, to my shock, I realized that the insurance unit talent manager blocked me to a useless opportunity so that the finance unit would not be able to map me.

There were email chains floating around between finance unit project managers, insurance unit talent manager, and finance unit talent manager. This is how it went. On Monday morning, finance unit project manager wrote something like below to finance unit talent manager:

> "Ramakrishna was mapped to another demand; he has already been selected by client after the interview. Kindly help here to map him to our demand."

On Monday afternoon, financial services unit talent manager said:

> "He is mapped to an insurance demand due to high bench. Hence I can't map him back."

I am sure she did not even know what she was talking about.

Next is our superhero from insurance talent management. He did not even know that I existed until that point. The insurance unit talent manager said:

> "Since we found an opportunity with insurance unit, currently he is mapped to the same demand."

How nice it would have been if he said, "Only after I received the email from finance unit, I shamelessly blocked the employee to a useless opportunity with insurance unit."

I called up the insurance unit talent manager and asked why he was not releasing me from insurance unit. He said, "You are now part of insurance unit. It's the process." Long story short: the emails went back and forth for three weeks without any result.

They wasted three weeks. Just for your background, the talent managers are not new employees. They are equivalent to senior managers.

It was a waste of time exchanging emails and doing follow-ups, and a waste of money from weeks of my unutilized resource time.

A technology company's delivery unit is the cash cow of the company. Instead of helping them, talent management team was sabotaging them. In the name of process, the talent managers were behaving like lunatics.

No one had the common sense to ask, "What's good for the company?" "What matters in the end?" or "Does the process really matter?"

When to change the process

Sometimes a one-off activity will take only one hour of manual effort. But in the name of process, if you spend another day trying to create a macro, then it is not going to help. Sometimes you need to use common sense and finish off your work.

The idea of having a process in place is to help you, and the company, get more done with less. We need to ask if the process is adding value, or helping us solve problems. And if it doesn't, it is time to change the process.

I want you to know what an ultra-successful tech CEO thinks about process. The following is an excerpt from the letter which Jeff Bezos, CEO and founder of Amazon, wrote to his employees and stakeholders: "Good process serves you so you can serve customers. But if you're not watchful, the process can become the thing. This can easily happen in large organizations. The process becomes the proxy for the result you want. You stop looking at outcomes and just make sure you're doing the process right. Gulp. The process is not the thing. It's always worth asking, do we own the process or does the process own us?"[7]

Simple tools and strategies

I have a MacBook Pro and an iPhone and I have a confession to make. I still struggle to use iTunes, and transfer songs from my MacBook Pro to any Windows or Android based devices.

Though I am a techie, that's how bad I am when it comes to use of apps. I am sure you love to install apps and use the latest gadgets. But how many apps are you using to get more done with less? The apps are usually pretty good, having more features than necessary. It's usually not an app that is the problem. It's usually the strategy— how to make it useful for our life—that is the problem.

If these simple tools and strategies can work for me, I am sure they can work for you as well.

Pen and paper

When doing creative work like designing, writing algorithms, solving data flow, or figuring out a test scenario, you need to map, or scribble, or just have a means to bring the thoughts and ideas out of your mind. Even though we are at the forefront of the technology, I believe pen and paper is still a pretty good tool.

For you skeptics, there is still lot of power in this good old tool. Why? Ideas are free flowing. We can visualize different pieces and form connections between them. We can quickly transfer ideas to our colleagues.

If you just can't stand the idea of a pen and paper, a whiteboard and marker is not bad. Take what works and run with it. At the end of the day, it should help you get more done with less, whether finding creative solutions or simplifying complex problems or doing both in less time.

Checklist

As the world is getting consumer-oriented, attention and focus are becoming scarce resources. Hence, our next strategy is to create checklists. Checklists are proven to be a powerful tool to get more done with less, and with more accuracy. Atul Gawande's bestselling book *Checklist Manifesto* clearly testifies to this point. A pen and notepad or your smartphone to-do list works well as a personal checklist manifesto.

The strategy is simple. Write down things as and when any to-do item comes to your mind. Then, when you get free time, get them done one by one, and more importantly cross them off. Make sure you don't overload with hundreds of things. About six to 10 tasks can do the magic. These tasks should not include daily chores like eating lunch or drinking water. You'll do that anyway. These should include the transient ones that help you grow in whichever area you'd like. You can use the notebook to track the small things that can be essential but you often miss. I find this pen and paper technique to be more helpful for my projects outside work. I use them to jot down ideas related to a book project, structure the book, or research a topic. And then cross it off once it is done.

This is helpful more as a transient device, rather than a permanent device. In techie terms, checklists should not be treated as a hard disk but rather as a pen drive. The usage is totally up to you. But remember: *Writing to-do items and manually crossing them out has a power.*

In fact, there is research that supports manual writing versus digital note taking. Pam A. Mueller and Daniel M. Oppenheimer wrote in *Psychological Science*, "The present research suggests that even when laptops are used solely to take notes, they may still be impairing learning because their use results in shallower processing. In three studies, we found that students who took notes on laptops performed worse on conceptual questions than students who took notes longhand."[8]

Personally, I have started using longhand writing for my to-dos and note taking. This has been immensely helpful for me, especially for catching ideas that come up before or after sleep, while traveling or talking to someone. Once you cross off the task using hand, *the sense of accomplishment and momentum to carry on the next task is just awesome.*

What works at work

What I have found is that creating a to-do list using Notepad (software application) is effective at work. This is effective when someone else assigns the tasks. What I aim for is to empty the notepad by the end of the day. I'll remove the task once it is over. For *work in progress* tasks, I'll just make a quick note of the status next to the task name.

In general, pen and paper to-do lists are effective when you are finishing any self-driven projects. Creating to-do list tasks in Notepad software application (or any simple software application) is effective for assigned work, such as when your boss or client is assigning some work to be completed by end of day.

During the written communication chapter, we'll learn more on how to leverage notepad to-do lists with our email client, such as Microsoft Outlook, for getting things to completion.

Now, let us talk about note taking.

Note taking

One area where I really suck is note taking, whether from a seminar, classroom, website, magazine, newspaper, or book. It never worked for me. Maybe I am bad at manual note taking, or maybe I am not disciplined enough to maintain the notebooks.

But I know, when done well, note taking can be a powerhouse of knowledge.

When I was a child, I used to cut different articles from the newspaper that were interesting. But, after a few years, I hardly referred to those cuttings. Why? It was hard to search for any information. It is a real time-suck to search when we actually need to refer back to our notes.

But there is hope. If I can solve this problem, I think anyone can solve it.

Recently, I started using an app and it has changed my life with respect to note taking. I highly recommend Evernote app (https://evernote.com/) because I found it to be a blessing for people like me. This app can capture anything and everything we can think and see.

We can create different notebooks. These notebooks can serve different projects that we are focusing on. Under a specific notebook, we can start collecting relevant notes. We can digitally write or draw. We can capture what we see on our mobile and computer screens (a caveat: don't store screenshots from restricted or data-sensitive workplaces), and send it to our Evernote account. We can take photos of articles that we are reading from newspapers or magazines and send them to our account. Since Evernote is cloud based, we can access the notes from anywhere using any device. The best and beautiful part is that all the notes are *searchable*. You can search for words even in your screenshots and pictures!

We have covered a lot of strategies in this chapter. If you feel overwhelmed, just start with one strategy. Once you are comfortable, and it becomes second nature to you, move to the next strategy.

If doing work is one thing, converting that work into words is another, which is what we'll see next.

KEY TAKEAWAYS

- Parkinson's Law says that work expands with the available time.

- Do light multitasking for non-creative tasks, and use the power of uninterrupted work for creative tasks.

- Priority should be our priority when starting work. Use the Eisenhower matrix to decide priority after dividing your tasks into Q1, Q2, Q3, and Q4 buckets.

- All hours are not the same. Your performance is at a peak only during certain hours, which is your active time. Use your active time for Q1 and Q2 tasks.

- Find the 20 percent of tasks, people, and resources that are leading to 80 percent of the results, and invest your time and energy in those areas.

- Follow up just before the deadline. Follow through to make sure that the work is progressing at the right pace so that it can complete on time.

- Process is not the thing. We need to use process to solve problems, complete work, and add value to our clients.

- Use pen and paper to take thoughts out of your mind. Use pen-and-paper to-do lists for personal projects. Use digital to-do lists for assigned work. Use Evernote or a similar app for permanent note taking.

CHAPTER 4

HOW TO WRITE EFFECTIVE EMAILS

In which, we'll learn: three important aspects of an email, four situations when we shouldn't write, five tools to get attention, how to handle typos, how to respond smartly, and how to get work done

I will never forget what my friend said while we were sitting in Starbucks. He is a program manager in one of the multinationals. We were catching up after several years. We were talking about life and work. I was enjoying the aroma of freshly brewed cappuccino but what he said caught my complete attention. He said, "It was really hard for me to digest. It took a lot of time to overcome the fact that my work boiled down to writing proper emails."

The invention of email in the information revolution seems like the invention of electricity of the modern era. It's just so powerful. Not just for a software techie, but also for a corporate professional or an entrepreneur, email-writing skills have become a must-have.

In the tech world, email is the most used medium of communication, yet very few employers test this skill while hiring. All things being equal in a candidate, the differentiator should be that that the guy or gal who writes better should be hired.

Writing well does not mean that the person is good with words. It shows that the person has developed clear thinking, and that is a very important trait for a techie.

Early in my career, my team lead gave me some feedback about my emails. She said, "You need to improve your writing. It can be more effective, use highlighters, bold, etc." I was a fresh trainee, full of energy. I took it as a personal challenge. In that burst of enthusiasm, I wrote the best email with rich words, using highlighters such as underline and color for all the important words.

I was rejoicing in anticipation of appreciation from my team lead. I went to her desk. The expression on her face said it all. She said, "It looks like every word in your email is important." Ouch, that was insulting. If you could have captured the look on my face, it would have been worth a million bucks.

But, you need to know what I did. I had highlighted words in red, blue, and green. I had underlined or boldfaced every other word. If you saw that email now, I bet you would roll out laughing on the floor.

But for someone like me, to get past that phase and now a write a book is not a small thing. I have learned some key things that helped me write better. And I want to share them with you.

Though I'll cover writing skills using email as the medium, the principles can be used in other areas such as document creation, status reports, or any other work where you need to type or write words.

The most important aspect of your email

Perhaps the most important aspect of your email (or any writing) is clarity. What you are writing *should make sense*. Is it clearly communicating what you want to tell?

After writing, read it aloud to check if it makes sense. That's the easiest way to catch clarity issues.

Now, let's understand the following three specific ideas to achieve clarity.

1. Have short paragraphs and proper spacing

Let us take these two writing samples.

Sample 1: When I was in high school, I always thought that "I should sharpen my programming skills and only then will I be a good software engineer." Though I was not comfortable with computers, I used to learn about different languages and equip myself.

Sample 2: When I was in high school, I always thought, "I should sharpen my programming skills. Only then will I be a good software engineer."

Though I was not a computer geek, I used to learn about different programming languages to equip myself.

Which one is better? Of course, it is Sample 2.

Nobody likes to read big paragraphs at work.

Big paragraphs are overwhelming and people don't have time to read long emails word by word. That's why we need to *have short paragraphs that have one big idea.* This helps the reader to understand one point at a time.

One more important aspect is to give proper spacing, so that it is easy to consume the information. It's much easier to read when you cap off to 60 or 70 percent of the entire width.

2. Use common, not complex words

Are you someone who catches everyone's attention because of your excellent vocabulary? But that's exactly what you shouldn't do in an email.

We work in a global economy and the proficiency levels of readers vary drastically. I could write, "Since its inception, our company has endeavored to be cognizant of the fact that employee proficiencies are important." Or I could write, "Since its start, our company has been aware of the fact that employee skills are important."

Which one is easy to read and understand? It's obviously the second one. Hence, don't use words that are complex. What's important is *using common words that convey what you mean*. This is not just for email but also for communication in general.

When it comes to business communication, simplicity always wins. Now that we have considered *style* and *words*, next we'll see *action*.

3. Have a clear call to action

Any email that you send should clearly tell *what you want the reader to do*. And also, it should tell *by when you want the reply*.

There are many fancy abbreviations such as FYI (for your information), FYA (for your action), ETA (estimated time of arrival), EOD (end of day) or ASAP (as soon as possible). Use them if you like, but make sure that you clearly state the action that you want the reader to take.

Preferably have one call to action. If it's more than one, then make it obvious that you need the reader's response to all the different calls to action. This can be achieved by sending the action items as numbered lists.

Now, that the basics are covered, let's take a step further.

Catching attention: Tools and scenarios

As the sender, we know the points that the reader should not miss. But often, we do not take the extra effort to make it easy for the reader to get it. Let us learn some simple tools that we can use to catch the reader's attention.

- Bold: Formatting the words to boldface helps to highlight titles. You can also use it for any specific words or sentences in your email.

- Underline: Formatting the words in underline helps for sub-titles. But you can also use it for any specific words or sentences in your email.

- Background color: Highlighting with yellow background color can be your default for sentences indicating important priority.

- Font color: Changing the font color to contrast during inline replies to an email works well. Use blue for normal situations and red for urgent situations.

- Capital letters: Often, words in all-capital letters are used to indicate abbreviations. Example: DC (development center). In general, writing a sentence in capital letters means you are shouting. It is disrespectful. That's why it is a strict NO. But a few words in CAPS can grab the attention of your reader. It is like a friendly shout. For example, observe the use of HOLD in the following statement: "Please put the job on HOLD for tomorrow's run."

A caveat: I want to warn against the overuse of these tools. Use them minimally to catch the attention of your reader. Maybe just start off using background color and font color. Once the usage becomes second nature, you can explore other attention-grabbing tools.

Let's see the usage of these tools.

When priority is important

Let us say that you are responsible for completing some testing within two weeks. However, you are not able to proceed because your upstream application team did not provide a file.

You can do the following things to proactively handle the scenario:

1. Write a suitable subject line. Use the word "important" in the subject. For example, <Important> XXX Testing on Hold for More than two days

2. Highlight the main point in yellow background. Something as shown below works well.

> (Subject) <Important> XXX Testing on Hold for More than two days
>
> Hi All,
>
> This is regarding the timeline impact for completing our testing. ...
>
> ....
>
> ....
>
> Our Testing is on HOLD for more than 2 days because File XXX is pending from application YYY for more than 2 days.
>
> Thanks

3. Keep your leads, managers, in CC so that they are apprised of the situation.

When priority is urgent

Let us say you are responsible for completing the build activities in a few weeks. However, you just came to know that the testing team resources got rolled off the project without proper lead time.

You can take the following steps to proactively handle the scenario:

1. Write a suitable subject line with "urgent" in the subject. For example, <Urgent> XXX Testing Team rolled off without Notification

2. Highlight the critical point of the email in red font. Something as shown below works well.

> (Subject) <Urgent> XXX Testing Team rolled off without Notification
>
> Hi All,
>
> This is regarding the XXX testing team resources who got rolled off without any notification.
>
> ....
>
> ....
>
> This is big risk to our ZZZ changes planned on MMDDYY.
>
> Please treat it as urgent and advise ASAP.
>
> Thanks

3. Mark all your stakeholders: your managers, the erring team's managers, and relevant stakeholders in CC of the email.

Four things you don't do with email

Now that we have seen the key things to do with email, let's learn about things that we shouldn't do.

When we talk in person, both our body language and vocal variation support our words. When we talk on a call, only vocal variation supports our words. But when we send email, it's just words. Hence, we need to be careful while writing emails.

Please follow the following four rules.

Don't use words with connotations

First of all, I want you to be clear on choice of words.

Unlike speaking, a word in an email does not carry body language or voice modulation with it. It only carries the purest meaning. The meaning of *connotation* is an idea or feeling, which a word invokes for a person in addition to its literal or primary meaning.

Words can have a proper literal meaning but give a totally different feeling. For example, the literal meaning of the word "escalation" is just a rise or move to the next level.

However, watch what happens when you use the word as follows:

> Hi All,
>
> The requirements are not clear. The business partner was not able to answer this. Hence the business analyst escalated the queries to the business head.
>
> Thanks

When you look at the email and see the word "escalated," the first feeling you get is that something is wrong here. But if you look closely, there is nothing wrong. Escalated is used in a literal way. However, we know that escalation has become an unofficial lingo that conveys, "You are screwed."

Hence it is a bad idea to use the word escalated even with a positive intent. Rather, "sent" is a better word as shown below.

> Hi All,
>
> The requirements are not clear. The business partner was not able to answer this. Hence the business analyst sent the queries to the business head.

> Thanks

After writing your email, just skim it once. If you feel that any part can lead to multiple interpretations, change the words so that there can be only one interpretation.

Don't write do-or-die words

Sometimes, there are instances where you need to say NO or push back your work.

For example, if you don't have time to add a new feature in two weeks and you are supposed to convey that, then don't write, "It cannot be done in two weeks." Such a reply becomes offensive and you end up hurting egos. When egos flare up, the whole work environment goes down the drain.

Instead of directly saying NO, *add reasons along with an indirect NO*. Something like the following is always a better response:

> Hi Janet,
>
> It will be really difficult to pursue this feature. Since we will be risking the quality of the product, we will not be able to complete the testing within the two-week time frame.
>
> Thanks
> Rama

Don't assume the complexity or priority for the reader

Let's say there is a code release tonight. To make a go or no-go decision, we want to get inputs from the enterprise release team. If the task only takes a few minutes, should we write?

Hi Tom,

Can you please let us know the timing for install downtime? It might only take a minute.

Thanks
Rama

If I write that, Tom will be thinking, "Who the heck (or any better word) is he to tell me how long it will take?"

We don't know how many such tasks Tom has, or if there is anything critical going on. Don't write that they should work on your task because it takes less time to complete or it is easy to do. There is a better way.

Always write *why you need it quickly* and *by when you need it (ETA)*.

A better way to rewrite the above example is,

Hi Tom,

Can you please get back on this by today 4 p.m.? We have a release scheduled for tonight. Your inputs are critical for us to make a decision on go or no-go.

Thanks
Rama

Don't write when you are upset

We get upset when we feel negative emotions. Negative emotions are intoxicating like alcohol. They can influence you to do things that you do not intend to do. You might use some really hard or foul words that can go very bad against you. And that's disastrous.

I agree that you can't be cool all the time. There are times when you might get emotional. Even if you are right and the other person is wrong, never write anything negative in an email. It's a big NO.

If you are not able to control your emotions, move out of your cubicle. I can't emphasize this enough. Never, ever sit in your cubicle when you feel negative.

Make an excuse and go home. Have a beer. Watch TV. Call your friend or girlfriend. Settle down. Think it through and regroup.

Never write anything in email that will show you as aggressive or negative. Email is more than a communication medium. Email is a storage and retrieval medium as well.

All our documents can collect dust but not our emails. Within a flash of a minute, anyone involved in your project or company can retrieve an email you wrote a few years ago. It'll act as a documentation and proof of your behavior. If there is any email that proves you were aggressive or negative, people can use it against you anytime later as well.

What good are these email skills, if we don't learn about the art of responding as well?

The art of responding to emails

Your email writing skills boil down to how thoughtfully you respond to emails. And that's why I have handpicked the most common scenarios:

Last in, first read

Years ago, I developed a habit of reading emails in the order of first in, first read. But I eventually ran into a problem with this approach. I was missing the latest emails on the same subjects. Sometimes, I even replied to the outdated email, which was embarrassing.

And that's why we should always read emails in the order of last in, first read so that you reply to the latest and current email.

Reply inline for multiple questions

Sometimes, the email that you received has multiple questions seeking your answers on each point. It will become really hard for you to reply through a fresh email because the reader might struggle to match your answers and the original questions.

And that's why you should leverage inline replies. Inline reply means you write down your answers—preferably using a different color—just below the original questions.

When to use Reply and when to use Reply All

Have you even thought of when to use Reply and when to use Reply All?

Case one: Someone sends an email only to you, and you use Reply. Sender is cool and you are cool. Sometimes the sender will not keep your boss in CC when asking your help. You need to voluntarily keep your boss in CC while replying to the email.

Case two: Someone sends you an email keeping five others in CC, and you still reply only to the sender. You are cool but sender might not be cool. There was a reason that the sender kept the people in CC. It is imperative that you use Reply All so that everybody is on the same page.

The strategy is: If someone is in CC when you receive the email, they should be in CC when you reply as well.

There might be an exception here. If you feel the folks in CC are not relevant anymore, and you think they need not know about your reply, then you can remove them from your reply.

When to use attachment, when not to use attachment

Have you ever wondered if you should use attachment in your email?

Many of your readers will not open an attachment unless really needed. So, stick to writing content in the body of the email. This is another way to make sure nobody in your recipient list misses your information.

Having said that, there are times you need to use attachment. Attachments are helpful when we want to include things such as an issue tracker, project status, a deliverable, or a flow chart. Use attachment only when really needed.

Correct the subject line

How many times have you been part of big email chains? There is no denying that long email chains help people to understand the context and the history.

But, many times the direction of the core issue changes but the original subject line never changes. Even worse, sometimes a totally different issue unrelated to the original issue continues in the email chain.

When you find that the issue being discussed has changed, then change the subject line to an appropriate one. If it makes sense to start a fresh email, then start one with only the necessary stakeholders in copy. This is also my next point.

Start fresh email

Once my business partner and I were going back and forth on a task. We had to update some data in the database. Finally, we agreed upon the data.

But, before we could update in the database, she asked me to get approval from another business partner as well. And I sent the note to the other business partner.

The next day, my business partner sent me a separate note,

> Hi Rama
>
> I have some feedback. The next time, kindly send a fresh email with only the data that needs to be approved ☺.
>
> Thanks

Ouch, that smiley was just added so that the blow was sweetened.

The mistake: I sent the email to the other business partner, on the top of the internal email chain.

My business partner was right. I should have sent a fresh email keeping only the needed data for approval. The other business unit head need not know what all we discussed internally.

And that's why you should be sending out fresh emails to people outside your team or project.

Handling email conflicts

Have you been part of long email chains, which happen as a result of mindless arguments between different people?

If you are ever part of either conflicting party, handle the situation based on the following idea. *If the same point is discussed with no direction even after three or four email exchanges*, it's time to take action. Conduct a useful meeting and resolve the issue. (We'll see how to conduct useful meetings in the next chapter.) You'll save a lot of time and effort for all the recipients.

We all know that to err is human. And that's why we also need know how to handle errors.

Handling typos after sending an email

Have you realized there were typos after you sent an email?

What do you do in such cases? First, you should see whether the typo is harmful or harmless.

Harmful means the typo changed the meaning of your statement. For example, I wrote, "The file is used in Job XXX" but I wanted to write, "The file is not used in Job XXX." There are options like Message Recall to handle such situations.

But doing a *Reply All* with the correction in red works best.

To fix the example, we just need to add "not" as a correction in red, and write something like this:

> Hi All
>
> My bad, small correction in red, "The file is not used in Job XXX."
>
> Thanks
> Rama

How about a harmless case, where the typo did not change the meaning of the sentence? For example, I wrote, "The file not used in Job XXX" but I wanted to write, "The file is not used in Job XXX." (I missed the word "is.") What do we do?

Nothing.

People are busy and they won't expect another email for trivial grammar issues or typos that do not change any meaning. They'll understand. However, make sure you do not keep repeating such typos.

The most important benefit of an email

What people say is not a data point, because it is not stored. However, what people write is a data point. Email is such a cool thing. It is a storage device. It is an archival device. But apparently, it works as a document of proof, which is its most important benefit. This reminds me of an incident.

In one of my earlier projects, there was a meeting between our application and interface application. They agreed on several points. Later, there was a production issue because the interface team messed up on one of our agreements.

Our team went off the client escalation because of the documented email that I had sent minutes after our alignment meeting.

You might have faced situations when folks need to confirm on a question or an assumption. They confirm on call or instant message but not over email. You might wait for few days before following up or forgetting about it.

A better way to handle such situations is as follows: Reply on top of the email chain or send a fresh email with the confirmation that you got on call or instant message.

> Hi Jane,
>
> Thanks for your time. As discussed, I am sending out the minutes of our discussion. Feel free to add any point, which I may have missed.
>
> [Point 1]
>
> [Point 2]
>
> Thanks
> Rama

If you are a corporate warrior, then email is your main weapon. For any alignment, agreement, discussion, or help, make sure that you document it using email. It does not mean that you don't trust them. You are just being cautious. Documenting things using email can really help you in many situations.

Finally, let's see how to use email as a productivity tool to get more work done.

Using email to get the work done

Till now, we saw email as a communication, storage, archival, and documentation device. If that's not enough, I'm going say that it can be used as a tracking as well as a prioritization device.

Looks like we don't need any project management software. And that's the truth. Many of us can just manage our work through an email client such as Outlook.

Remember, we discussed creating checklists using Notepad. But that was the second step. The first step is to filter the work that we are supposed to do. The strategy is:

1. Create a *Rule* in your email client to *flag* all incoming emails. You can do a lot more with Rules. Please explore this option if you need advance optimization.

2. Clear emails in batches. Browse through them, and un-flag them when the email is not relevant to you or you don't need to take any action, or if you can do a quick reply. This way, you'll only end up having flagged items that you'll really need to work on and reply to.

3. Copy those items onto a notepad and create a checklist of to-do items for the day.

4. Once you complete—usually marked by the ritual of sending an email—the main tasks, you can un-flag the corresponding email.

You can take this a step further by using different flags, marked by different colors, for Q1 (urgent and important), Q2 (important and not urgent), Q3 (not important and urgent), and Q4 (not important and not urgent) tasks.

If the to-do items do not finish by the end of the day, you can send an email to yourself with the subject line "to do for 09/21" where 09/21 will be tomorrow's date. This means that you have a list of items ready to attack when you log in the next day.

When I joined the client location as the technology lead, I had to handle five different application systems comprised of three different business units and three different technology managers. It was tough. I am not even talking about the complexity of the work. The mere position of being the face of so many different stakeholders was a challenging job. I was getting like 100 to 200 emails per day. I was getting buried in emails. It was more like the full day went in receiving and sending emails. I hardly had any time to look into the issues.

My then lead came to check out how I was doing. He saw my plight and taught me some strategies to clear emails in batches.

1) Escalate to get quick responses. (*Do this based on situation and circumstance.*)

2) If you don't know an answer, ask for clarifications and buy more time.

3) Delegate any work (even small) that your subordinates can do.

Use the above rules to clear as many emails as possible off your plate. You can set a time of 20 or 30 minutes per day in the morning and 20 minutes per day in the afternoon and clear your emails.

This way you'll get more done with less using email.

In this chapter, we saw how to write effective emails but as the tech world is slowly shifting away from waterfall to agile methodology, oral communication has become even more critical. And that's what is coming next.

KEY TAKEAWAYS

- Clarity is the most important aspect of any email. Write short paragraphs that have ONE main idea. Give proper length to your sentences. Have a clear call to action. Use common words that convey the meaning of what you want to communicate.

- Don't use words that have different connotations and do-or-die words. Don't decide the complexity or priority on behalf of the reader. And never write email when you are upset.

- Use formatting tools such as bold, italics, underline, background highlight, font color, and capital letters (only for specific words) to catch the attention of your reader. Start with a few, and make it second nature.

- If a typo changes the meaning of email, send a follow-up email with the correction. If the typo does not change the intended meaning, do not send any follow-up email, but make sure you do not repeat the mistake.

- Email is a documented proof. Have all the key discussions and alignments documented in an email.

- Check emails in the order of last in, first read. Reply inline for multiple questions. Use *Reply* to sender. Use *Reply All* to copy recipients in CC. Use attachment sparingly. Start fresh emails when sending emails to new areas. Be quick to set up a meeting if there are email conflicts.

- Flag all incoming emails, use to-do checklist for tasks that take time, and clear emails in batches.

CHAPTER 5

SPEAK SENSE INTO YOUR LISTENERS

In which, we'll learn: role-play, expression, reflection, intelligibility, simplicity, 10 nuggets to conduct useful meetings and five secrets to help stakeholders take a decision

The word "communication" has become cliché. Have you heard people say, "You need to improve your communication skills?" But quite often, nobody will give specific areas of improvement.

If we want to improve, we need to be specific.

- Are we articulating well? To be specific, are we able to speak clearly, fluently, and coherently?

- Are we intelligible? To be specific, are people able to understand what we are saying?

- Are we able to simplify things? To be specific, are we able to convey complex concepts in simple terms?

- Are we talking sense in meetings? Are we able to conduct and drive useful meetings?

- Are we able to persuade? To be specific, are we helping our stakeholders make a decision?

We'll deal with all the above questions. But before that, let's conquer fear of speaking.

Overcoming fear of speaking

I have observed if *skill* increases performance, then *fear* decreases performance. And one of the main fears is fear of speaking at any critical juncture. You'll mainly feel this when you talk in a critical meeting or you work one on one with critical stakeholders. And that's why I want to recommend this simple three-step process.

1. Prepare using role-play

One strategy that works pretty well for preparation is doing role-play. Anticipate the potential questions that the stakeholders might have and then answer those questions. Ask your friend or partner to do the role-play with you. It's fun as well.

I remember going into an empty conference room to practice the sentences that I was going to speak in a critical meeting. This strategy has helped me a number of times.

2. Express yourself

Have you been in a meeting, sitting in a corner and thinking, "When will this end? I wish I could get out of here soon." Most probably, everyone else in the room is thinking the same way. Before anyone can blabber and waste everyone's time, use that opportunity to express yourself.

You don't need to be an extrovert or a chatterbox to express yourself. In fact, you should speak less. As the famous Greek philosopher Plato said, "Wise men talk because they have something to say; fools, because they have to say something."

Your stakeholders will easily find out if you fake it. Remember, the goal is to express and add value. Not to make a fake impression.

What are some of the points that can be expressed?

You can speak about the pain points in the team or project, or ideas to improve the process (remember we discussed process is not the thing). Don't just raise concerns but also suggest some tentative solutions. Everyone raises concerns. Only a few will come up with solutions. Be in that few.

3. Reflect on every experience

Take the time to reflect on every experience by asking what went right, what went wrong, and how to speak better next time. You will not always speak perfectly, but if you reflect on your prior experience and keep at it, you will evolve and eventually get better and better. So do not worry about what people will think of you, think about how you will learn from your mistakes and speak well at the next opportunity.

In this section, we saw a simple game plan to grow out of speaking fear. Now, let's take it one step ahead, and learn the nuances while dealing with different stakeholders.

Speak to your listener's role

If you want to communicate something, will you use the same words to your clients, your boss, and your internal team?

What I am trying to say is that we need to speak in a way that makes sense to the roles that people are playing.

Let us say that your process failed in production environment where the software is LIVE. Would you say, "The job XYZ123 failed in production because the DB2 SQL return code -811 was not handled" to your client head?

You can but in my opinion, you shouldn't. You can say that to your internal team or even your boss but not your client.

If the client is a business user who has some level of technical knowledge, you can say something like, "The address validation job failed because we did not handle a database condition." But what if the stakeholder is part of senior management?

We need to speak in a way that'll answer what the listener is looking for. The primary concern of a senior level stakeholder (at your company or at the client end) is not *what caused the issue*. The primary concern is *when will the issue be resolved*. Hence, say, "There was an issue in the address validation job during the implementation. We are working on priority to resolve the issue."

The higher the position of the stakeholder, the more abstract your details should be. Abstraction might sound controversial. But, here, the situation is different because your stakeholder might not know the technical terms.

If they need more information, they'll anyway ask you more questions. But remember to start off at a level that'll make sense to them.

What I am saying is, think about your listeners' role and current experience level. Then, use words and details that'll make sense to them.

While speaking to your stakeholder, make sure you keep the following things in mind.

Be intelligible

"Intelligible" means *able to be understood*. Though it sounds very simple, it is a cornerstone of an effective communication process. What it means is that we should not just say, "I spoke. It's not my problem if the other person did not get it."

As my mentor Jerry Aiyathurai taught, we should say, "It's my responsibility as a speaker to make sure that a hundred percent of what I am saying is also the same hundred percent that the listener is understanding."

To achieve this, you need to improve your voice modulation and clarity. From a voice perspective, make sure it is clear without any mumbling, loud enough, and paced appropriately.

One of the major hurdles for intelligibility is accent.

If you have an accent that's different from that of your peers, you don't need to change it altogether. You'll get caught up with the accent, and then lose authenticity and confidence over the content.

Though I did not face any issues at work, I faced an issue while competing at higher levels in speech contests. Some people gave feedback that my accent was hard to follow. I worked with a speech coach and she helped me with a lot of things, but the strategy is this: *Speak slowly and clearly.* The idea is to speak slowly and clearly enunciate the words. This has worked well for me.

Likewise, if you are not able to follow someone else's accent, I'd recommend a simple hack. Try to get hold of the speaker's recorded voice, and then listen to it again and again. You'll slowly tune in to their accent. If you don't get hold of the speaker's recorded voice, it is still fine. After a few conversations, you'll be able to tune in. Just be patient and alert during the conversations.

Keep it simple

The world tries to make things complex. Maybe complexity is confusing, and what is confusing is sexy... which is a BS concept. I used to buy this BS concept for a long time. There were some folks who used to say things that sounded like, "I did a 5000 lines coding to run some program that will shake this building."

Earlier, people talked about cool things they did using.net, C#, or Java. Now, people talk about UX, UI, Java scripts, PERL, big data, DevOps, or cloud computing. I'll tell you one thing—anything new that your brain tries to process will seem complex.

Not because it is actually complex, but because our brain is fearful of the unknown.

If you willingly went to learn something from a training session, and after five minutes find yourself yawning, then it's not your problem. It's the person giving the information who is making it complicated.

"Simplicity is the ultimate sophistication." Before you think further, I did not say that, it was said by the genius Leonardo da Vinci. Simplifying things is complex! And it takes a great deal of skill to present things in a simplified way. Since many would not take the extra effort, you'll stand out when you simplify things.

Speaking is a much different ball game than written communication. While listening, how many chances do you get to understand the speaker? Only one chance! Your listener cannot keep saying, "Say that one more time" again and again. Hence, use simple words to serve your clients, or any other listener.

In fact, big-tier companies such as Aetna and Cigna have run several campaigns to persuade their employees to use simple words to communicate with their customers. Why would they invest money on such seemingly simple initiatives?

Well, because it is critical for their business. Perhaps it is critical for you and me as well. Your listeners and clients will judge you based on how much sense you make; not how many fancy words you use.

Now that we've seen the nuances of speaking to our stakeholders, let's see how to conduct useful meetings, that one thing which we would love to hate.

Conduct useful meetings

Though meetings have a bad rap of not being useful, they are very helpful provided they are conducted in a useful manner. Meetings are needed for things that require collaboration and discussion, which emails cannot do.

As a prerequisite, I would recommend that you talk to your manager or respective IT team to arrange for a bridge number (a common dial-in number where folks can join from anywhere in the world) and screen-sharing tool exclusive for you.

This will give you the autonomy to conduct meetings without depending on anyone else. The following nuggets will definitely help you conduct useful meetings.

Choosing venue

If all the participants are co-located near your workstation, then try to have the meeting at the workstation. This will avoid the transfer cost between the workstation and the conference room.

Conduct in-person conference room meetings only when really needed. If it's a distributed environment, which is the case these days, you can always conduct a virtual meeting using a dial-in bridge and screen-sharing tool.

Have clear agenda

Conduct the meeting only if you have a clear agenda. Otherwise you'll end up wasting everyone's time. Set clear expectations using the agenda. You don't need to beautify and send the agenda. Just simple pointers as shown below will do.

Hi All,

We'll be discussing the following issues.

- *Item A*

- *Item B*

- *Item C*

Thanks

If nothing else, the agenda should convey what is going to be discussed during the meeting.

Invite necessary participants

Invite only necessary people who can contribute. Unnecessary people can be included in copy when sending the minutes of the meeting.

And one more important thing is: *You need to follow through whether the key participants are going to join*. Usually they accept your invite. If they don't, email them, ping them, or talk to them beforehand to make sure that they're going to join your call.

Buffer before beginning

Give two to three minutes of buffer before you begin your meeting. If you are conducting the meeting over a virtual conference call, announce the attendee names so that everyone knows who else is on call.

Before meetings begin, while waiting for others to join, there is a tendency for people to chitchat about personal things. If stakeholders are talking, you too should join in the small talk. Why? These are small windows of opportunities for building rapport. But, transition into official topics at the first chance.

For example, if two or more participants are well known to each other, they might start off with their own agenda about how they spent their weekend. If that happens, say, "Even I went to this place [replace 'place' with your specific activity] and it was awesome. Janet [replace 'Janet' with your stakeholder name], I have a quick question for you about the customer file [replace 'customer file' with your topic]?"

Please observe how we got into work-related matters without hurting anybody. Use this buffer time to clarify any quick issue with specific participants.

Initiate dialogue

If you are driving the meeting, make the people joining the call comfortable. Say something like, "Hi Mike. How you doing?"

If someone asks you, "Hi Rama. How you doing?" they are not expecting you to give the actual answer. Just say, "Good, thanks." And move on to the heart of the meeting.

Don't allow change of direction

I don't know if it's just me. I am sure you might have noticed that there is always one sucker who will pitch and keep talking about irrelevant things.

Please don't allow that to happen.

If anyone interrupts the flow and seems to change the direction of the meeting, interrupt and say, "Hi John [replace 'John' with the sucker]. Sorry to interrupt. We are discussing point A right now. We'll come to your point pretty soon. Tom [replace 'Tom' with your stakeholder], can you please continue on point A [replace 'point A' with the topic of discussion]?"

Call out disturbances

If you have joined through dial-in bridge, which is quite common these days, then there could be disturbances. If someone's voice is not clear, call it out in a polite manner.

If you are hearing background noise, it might be because participants forget to put their phones on mute. In that case, just say, "If you are not speaking, please go on mute."

Resolve hearing issues

Sometimes, people speak low or not near the microphone of their phone. If you are unable to understand what the speaker is saying on the call, in a polite manner, say something like, "I am not sure if it's just me. I am having a hard time hearing Jack [replace 'Jack' with the name of the actual person]."

If that's a common problem, someone else will second you and the other speaker will take corrective action. If not, someone else will say that the line is clear. In that case, the problem could be at your end. Check your phone receiver or dial in from a different phone if necessary.

Show and solve

Meetings are criticized as waste of time because people just talk, and talk, and talk without any concrete progress of work. That's why it's not wise to talk abstractly. If you are in a virtual meeting, show the visuals using a screen-sharing tool such as WebEx or Live Meeting.

People should see stuff so that they can offer correct solutions rather than *assume* something else. The not so politically correct definition for the word "assume" is "make an ass out of you and me."

Give back more time

Sometimes the meeting ends before the scheduled time. Even though the meeting was scheduled for 30 minutes, if all agenda items end in 10 minutes, don't add new agenda items unless they are critical. End the call and say, "Happy to give back 20 minutes."

If agenda items do not end even after the whole duration of the meeting, then there are two ways you can handle this.

One: if there are only a few items, and it is critical to close them, say, "Just a quick second. We are going on top of the hour. If everybody is okay, can we spend five more minutes to discuss the remaining few items as well?"

Two: if the few items are not critical, then you say something like, "Just a quick second. We are going on top of the hour. Let's discuss the remaining items in the next meeting."

Send the minutes of the meeting

After the meeting, sending the minutes, including the key discussions that happened, helps everyone be accountable. Things agreed on call are 99 percent of the times taken for granted, especially if it is the other person's need. Not just that, having this documented helps as proof of what was aligned and why certain decisions were taken.

You don't need to write big paragraphs. Just make sure that you mention participants who attended the meeting, the agreements, and the action items.

For example:

Hi All,

Thanks for joining in and contributing.

Participants: Tom, Jamie, Ravi, and Janet.

Minutes of meeting and Action Items:

1. We aligned that Tom will complete the code migration by tomorrow (09/01) EOD. Jamie agreed to support Tom if there are any issues.

2. Jamie and Ravi will work on solving the email tracking issue.

Please add any other points if needed.

Thanks

In this section, we saw how to conduct useful meetings. But, the whole purpose of any meeting is to arrive at decisions, which is what we'll see next.

Help in decision-making

Most of the speaking that we do in the tech world boils down to someone making that damn decision. And yet, what's rather sad is, instead of focusing on making that decision, people keep talking and talking and talking. In other words, things keep getting dragged and dragged and dragged.

I would not say that it is a fault of any one role. I believe decision-making is a collective game. Though the decision-making power is usually held by the project sponsor (the one who pays for the project or runs the project), I think techies play a key role in helping the stakeholder take a decision.

Let's take an illustration. You are involved in a requirement discussion with your superiors or clients. You realize that the discussion is not making any sense. Will you say, "We should not do it" or will you say, "No problem, we will do it"?

The first option is being aggressive. The second option is being passive. Both the approaches are not advisable. What is advisable is being *assertive*.

Assertiveness means expressing thoughts, feelings, and beliefs in direct, honest, and appropriate ways. And that's the reason why you should give reasons and express feelings and thoughts in a genuine way but not take any decision on their behalf. The final decision is for the stakeholder to take. Remember, you are just the solution provider.

Let's continue the scenario. How about saying, "It seems this functionality [replace 'functionality' with actual functionality name] is not adding any value for our objective [replace 'objective' with the actual objective] because of X [X is the reason why you think it is not needed]. Just wanted to know your thoughts on this."

And then wait till the other person responds. (Golden rule of negotiation: After the pitch, the one who speaks first loses leverage.) The other person will give an answer.

If that's not clear, get a crystal-clear answer by asking, "Just to reiterate, are we saying that we don't need to pursue this functionality further?" And then wait till the other person responds. By doing this, you are making the other person responsible for the decision.

Let's understand the key strategies to keep in mind while persuading our stakeholders to take any decision.

Be assertive in your approach

If your stakeholders are not able to take a clear decision, then you need to explore further by asking why they are not giving a clear answer.

Keep in mind that every further probe should be in an assertive tone. It should not push others. Sometimes, even after you trying, your stakeholder might not agree to your view.

Politely and respectfully, say that you differ with the decision because of such and such reason, but commit to the final decision.

Give space for the stakeholder

The best speakers are not just the ones who speak well but also the ones who pause and listen. That's why we need to wait after asking a question.

One of the main problems in any discussion is that people just keep talking back and forth. If you just give people *the space to think, reflect, and talk it out*, they'll love working with you.

Collective responsibility

Always use words such as "we" or "our" instead of "you" or "I." This is a powerful strategy because you'll make everyone feel as if the decision is collective instead of a one-person decision.

One interpretation

Most stakeholders are smart. They'll say what they want but never say anything in black and white. They'll allow you to interpret. And that's not good.

All the parties must agree and hence it's your responsibility to make sure that the final decision is clear for everybody. If it's a YES or NO type decision, then you and everyone involved in the discussion should be on the same page.

Be certain

During my first performance review, my line manager said, "I have observed that many times you don't seem to be sure of things." And I heard another voice, "I agree." That was my line manager's manager connected by phone.

I was fortunate to get honest feedback so that I could improve upon this aspect for the rest of my career. But during the performance review, I was not that good.

I was thinking, "You both were morons. Couldn't you tell me this when I said things that were uncertain? Do you need to wait six months so that you can add it as a weakness during performance review?"

In today's software tech world, knowing what the current code base is doing is a big challenge. Analyzing the existing code base is a huge skill. Not just that, there will be many decisions that will be made because of what inputs you give.

Be certain about one thing rather than doubtful about many things.

When you say something, always back your statement with facts or proofs. I agree, you might want to say something that will keep you on the safer side, but make sure what you say is *certain* so that your stakeholder can make a decision.

In this chapter, we learned about speaking sense into our listeners, but speaking also manifests into presenting when you want to educate more people either virtually or in-person. I'm pretty excited to share a simple system that can take your presentations to the next level. And that's what we'll be covering in the next chapter.

KEY TAKEAWAYS

- Find specific areas of improvement. Overcome speaking anxiety by preparation, expression, and reflection.

- Talk to your listeners based on their roles and experience levels. Be intelligible so that your listeners understand what you are saying. Use simple words.

- Conduct useful meetings by having a clear agenda, inviting necessary participants, giving buffer before starting the meeting, not allowing change of direction, calling out distractions, showing and solving, giving back time, and sending minutes of the meeting.

- Help in the decision-making process by being assertive, leading to one interpretation, taking collective responsibility, giving space to stakeholders, and being certain of what you are saying.

CHAPTER 6

A SIMPLE SYSTEM TO SUCCEED
WITH PRESENTATIONS

In which we'll learn how to: find purpose, do audience research, create an outline, make a solid slide deck, practice, overcome last-minute anxiety, handle Q&A, tackle glitches, and process feedback

"I thought that giving a speech was like reading an article and if you think that it's what it is, then, you just get up and read your article. Once you actually know that it is a world that has its own rules and principles, you are really acting. Then you are like, Oh, Wow. I got to throw myself into it in a significant way, and that's what I try to do," said Malcolm Gladwell, keynote speaker and author of five *New York Times* bestselling books, to fellow author Tim Ferriss during a podcast interview. [1]

In today's world, even as a techie, having presentation skills is not an option. It is a mandate because you'll need them for all kinds of things: knowledge-sharing sessions, delivering design walkthrough sessions, or pitching new ideas to potential clients.

There is no denying that the world is getting digital. So there is less physical and more virtual interaction. But the fundamental concepts for in-person or virtual presentations are the same, which is what we'll cover here. And I have addressed the difference when needed.

A presentation's success is directly proportional to the *amount of preparation*, whether it is an in-person presentation or a virtual presentation.

Even if you have read my books or other work related to public speaking, I highly recommend that you pay attention to these steps. If you follow the steps outlined here, you'll be able to crack even an in-person presentation outside your work. I have personally tested them and they work like a charm. I promise that these will be some of the most effective and actionable steps you have ever heard.

Find the purpose

Dev is a techie handling a key application for a banking client. On a Friday afternoon, his boss Tom came to him and said, "In Monday's client town hall, you are going to present the changes planned for next release."

Dev was excited. This was the opportunity he was looking for to make a mark. He even canceled his weekend outing with his girl-friend. He prepared a beautiful deck of PowerPoint slides.

On Monday morning, just 10 minutes before the meeting, Dev felt something was wrong. He felt someone came near him, got under his skin. He turned left to find no one. He turned right to find no one. But he heard a whisper in his ear, "Dev. Don't mess this up." He became terrified, his stomach got upset, his hands started to shake, and his legs started to wobble.

Dev seemed out of position. His excitement "to make a mark" changed to the anxiousness of "what if I mess this up?"

Amid all this, from behind him, he heard a voice say, "Are you ready?" He frantically turned around, only to find his boss Tom.

Looking at the petrified face of Dev, Tom started thinking, "Why do my folks always get scared of me? After all, I am not that bad of a boss."

The presentation started. Dev started with low energy and ended with even lower energy. He completed an overall mediocre presentation.

Dev was very disappointed with himself because he knew that he could have done way better. Dev wanted to do better. He went to his colleague, who said, "Dev, you need to prepare better." Then, he asked his friend. His friend said, "Dev, just overcome your fear." Finally, he asked his girlfriend. She said, "Baby, don't give such presentations again."

This was bothering Dev—his poor presentation, not his girlfriend's advice.

On the following Friday, he was sitting in the company cafeteria still trying to find the reason for his poor performance. His earlier boss Mr. Patrick from operations passed by.

Patrick is one of the best presenters in Dev's company. Dev said, "Hi Patrick." Patrick said, "Hey Dev. What's up with you?" After a few other exchanges, Dev said, "Pat, I really sucked at the presentation this week. I think I did everything right. But I am not sure why I sucked." Their conversation continued like this:

Pat: "Let me ask you something. Did you take time to really think WHY you were giving the presentation?"

Dev: "Well, I wanted to make a mark with the CFO."

Pat: "That's just the effect. But, did you try to find out WHY you were really doing the presentation. In other words, what was the purpose of the talk?"

Dev: «Well... I am not sure. Was it to update on the functionality planned for next release?"

Pat: "No, Dev. You need to clearly understand the purpose of your talk. That's the first thing you need to decide."

Have you felt nervous like Dev during a presentation? I suppose many of us do.

But the real secret to crushing the fear is to understand the WHY behind that talk. This is also relevant to life at large. Finding the WHY that excites you brings clarity, which in turn overcomes your anxiety. It'll help you clarify the PURPOSE.

For any public speaking scenario, someone has a need. In most cases, someone will invite you to speak. This person is called the presentation planner. Even if that's your boss (as in Dev›s story), he or she is playing the role of a presentation planner.

The presentation planner is a presenter's ally.

The more WHYs you ask the planner, the easier it is to find the purpose of the presentation. Ask, "Why do we need this presentation?" They might say, "We need to empower our staff to release the new product within one month."

Sometimes, you might not get a direct answer for your WHY. In that case, get into the planner's shoes and think about the possible reasons the talk will be useful for the planner and the audience. Talking about the audience, they are the very reason any presentation exists.

So, it makes sense to know about them.

Know your audience

Delivering the right product before the wrong people will not make a sale. During a typical presentation, you might not sell any product as such but the audience still needs to buy your sentences, one after the other. Only then will you have a chance to keep them engaged throughout your presentation.

During the Tim Ferriss podcast,[2] I heard Malcolm Gladwell talk about his public speaking philosophy. Tim asked, "You are a good public speaker, how do you plan your keynotes?" Malcolm said something that was like gold. He said, "I spend most of the time thinking who am I speaking to."

What Malcolm meant was that he spends most of the time trying to understand WHO his audience is. This is the mark of a professional. As Malcolm continued in the interview, he said he wouldn't speak to a set of IT specialists the same way he'll speak to a regular crowd. He would strive to bridge the gap between him and his audience.

So, how do we know our audience?

We need to find out whether they are techies, business folks, senior level leaders, managers, or a mixed crowd. And then, find the current knowledge levels and commonality among the audience. We need to find out their common needs, wants, desires, and fears.

Find *experiences* from your personal life that could relate to those needs, wants, desires, and fears. This will bridge that gap between you and your audience.

Knowing your audience before you speak is going to be your guiding point for the entire presentation process. But in particular, it helps during the content creation process.

Write your script

Joe is a natural speaker. Joe speaks really fluent English and outsmarts anyone with his presence of mind. But there is one problem. He never prepares the content for a presentation. He just wings it. This is not just Joe's problem. It's a common problem.

Folks do not prepare and end up giving a boring and cluttered presentation. It is a lot of wasted hours for all the attendees. All this could be avoided, if the presenter would allocate some time to *write or at least outline the content of the presentation*. Most people misunderstand this, and I'll clarify in a minute.

Before that, I want to tell you how to go about creating content. Spend some time thinking about all the relevant stories, facts, and illustrations that will support the presentation's WHY (purpose) and WHO (audience). Once you identify them, write them down. After that, try to fit these stories, facts, or illustrations into an outline.

Some of the outlines (or structures) that work well for techies are:

- SOAR (Situation, Objection, Action, and Results)

- Who (audience), What (topic), Why (its importance), How (the way it works)

- What, So What, Now What ("What" is the topic name)

Now, let's understand the misunderstood part. The goal of *writing* is not for *reading* it out or *memorizing* the content. The goal of *writing* is for IMPROVISING the content.

If you put your thoughts on paper and look at it after few days, I am sure, you'll think, "Oh... that does not make sense." And a light bulb might turn on. You'll get a beautiful idea. You'll be able to rewrite in a much better way.

I can tell you this. You cannot write the fifth version of the draft the first time. And to get to the fifth version, you need to start writing the first version.

The following might be out of context for a techie, but it is best example I can think of. Lincoln's Gettysburg Address is still being talked about even after more than a century. One main reason is that the masterpiece was written and rewritten multiple times. I'm not telling that you need to spend a lot of time perfecting the presentation like Abraham Lincoln. All I am saying is getting into the habit of writing things down and improving it will make your presentation way better.

PowerPoint slide deck has become a synonym for a presentation these days. I am not a big proponent of using a presentation deck unless it is absolutely needed. But in today's tech world, learning to create a presentation deck that does not suck is an essential skill, and that's what we'll see next.

Create a slide deck that doesn't suck

Now, let's talk about creating a slide deck. You might like Keynote (hello, Mac fan). But, for the sake of familiarity or popularity, I'll refer to PowerPoint as the presentation tool. Before deciding to use a slide deck, you should explore other options such as marker and whiteboard or marker and chart paper, and then select the option that suits your situation and need.

PowerPoint for any kind of a presentation stint has become like a gun to a policeman. Say the PowerPoint deck does not work during a presentation. The presenter might feel threatened by the audience, the way a policeman would feel with a faulty gun amidst criminals.

How many presentation decks have you seen that suck? Judging from the PowerPoints I have seen, a lot of them have bad design. The concept may be good, but it's often the small design changes that can transform such presentations. I am sure you know how to create a slide deck. But, I want to show some simple yet effective design strategies that'll at least make sure that your slide deck won't suck. Here we go:

Selecting font & background

Fonts and backgrounds are the backbone of your presentation, something the audience will see till the end. So it makes sense to understand nuances around their usage. Let's talk about font color, font types and size.

Color

Select font color based on the branding color of your company or website. If you are in corporate, templates should be there. Start there but remember the contrasting rules discussed below.

Contrast is what describes the relationship between fonts and background. And the color helps define this relationship. Hence, the font color and the background color of the slide should contrast with each other.

For example, use a white font on a black background or black font on a white background. The question is, "When should I use the first option and when should I use the second option, or does it matter at all?"

Yes, it matters.

Using a white font on a black background suits a darker room, when the room lighting is low. Black font on a white background suits a well-lit room. I used black and white as examples. But this works for any color contrasting pairs.

Now that the air around color is cleared, let's look at strategies to select font type and its size.

Font type and size

Have you seen different fonts littered around a slide deck? *I know, it sucks.*

The fact is many different font types distract your audience and give them a bad experience. The better option is to select two different font types. One is for headings, one for running text. That's it. In an exceptional case, go for a third font type.

If you are short of time, then do not change the default font settings of the PowerPoint tool. The default setting won't screw up your presentation. The Calibri family is the default. Calibri (heading) is used for headings. Default font size is 60, which is fine. Calibri (body) is used for running text. Default size is 28, which is fine for a virtual presentation. But for a boardroom presentation, make it 40. Font size matters in providing visibility to your audience. You have no idea how many presentations suck because of poor visibility.

If you are changing the fonts for the sake of being different, you might just screw things up. If you really want the deck to be different, then let's learn a little about fonts. There are generally three font types: serif, sans serif, and script. Serif fonts have extending "feet" at the ends of each character, while sans serif fonts do not. Script fonts use curly letters.

Do you know which font type is the best?

The best practice is to use sans serif fonts, especially for tech presentations. Jo Mackiewicz from Iowa State University conducted a study of font types.[3] This study examined 10 common and popular fonts displayed in projected PowerPoint text slides. Five had a sans serif font, and five did not. It investigated 37 participants' ratings of the fonts on four variables:

1) comfort of reading

2) professionalism

3) interest

4) attractiveness

And do you know which font did well?

Gill Sans, a popular sans serif font, was rated highly on each of the four variables. Gill Sans or a derivative should be available in both Mac and Windows. So don't ponder over choices and waste time. I have checked it out and it's pretty good. It's sleek, clear, and not many would know it. And that's why your presentation will stand out!

Using image

I am sure you have heard the age-old saying, "A picture is worth a thousand words." And you know what, it is right, especially when it comes to preparing a slide deck.

Having said that, do not include pictures for the sake of including them, but use them when you want to explain a complex idea.

For example, you can take pains to explain the Internet ecosystem through your speech or just plug in a picture of the Internet eco-system and do the talking while the audience can see the picture in front of them.

I'll cover the best practices for using images:

- Try selecting stock images that have a transparent back-ground. If you do not have a transparent background for the selected image, select quality images that do not lose pixel quality when you expand the image. Instead of keeping the image like a box on the floor, spread it like a carpet covering the floor.

- Place the key portion of the image (let's say a person or a data table) by using *thirds*. Let me explain thirds. Imagine di-viding the slide into three vertical parts and placing the key portion in the third part from the right or left so that there is space for text. This is a photography principle. Highly skilled photographers take their shots in thirds because the eyes are always drawn to the sides. Moreover, from our slide design perspective, it helps because you have two parts of the slide layout to write your text.

- If the image does not have open space where you can write the text, decrease the opacity of that portion and then write the text.

Representing data

If there is one major problem that's lingering in the tech space, it is storage of the gargantuan amounts of data generated every second. In a business context, there will be lots of data to present. So, we need to present data that will make sense to our audience.

Here are some simple strategies to represent data in a slide deck.

- Do not use tables consisting of data points. It will be hard for the audience to understand. Instead, *visualize the data* in terms of charts. Bar charts work well for most cases.

- Make sure you *highlight the portion* (with contrasting color) in the chart where you want the audience to focus.

Layering different elements

Let's say a presenter is explaining how the data flow is happening from one application (call it A) to another (call it B). The presenter has the entire flow on the slide. And the presenter is explaining the flow by asking the audience to specifically focus on A, then B, and so on.

How nice it would be if the audience can only see A, and as the presenter finishes talking about A and starts to talk about B, they see B, and then see an arrow in between A and B that represents the data flow.

Imagine the difference in your audience's experience.

There are no distractions; they see only what the presenter is currently discussing. They follow better because the flow is good. And they are attentive because there is this anticipation of what comes next.

To achieve this, you just need to do one more step after creating your slide. After you design the slide, *make sure you layer the different elements* as per your flow of the speech.

Elements could be sentences, arrows, pictures, or the entire bullet point list. An entire three-sentence bullet point list can be an element or each sentence of the bullet point list can be an element. The secret is to select the elements in a way that matches the flow of your speech.

Let's use the three-bullet point list as an example. We want the points to appear one by one. Here are the steps to create this layering in PowerPoint.

1. Go to *Animations* tab in MS PowerPoint.

2. Select first bullet point.

3. Check for "Entrance effects" tab.

4. Select *Fade* option. This is a classic option. There are many others but *Fade* option looks professional and hence it is recommended.

5. Now, select the second bullet point and repeat steps 3 and 4.

6. Then, select the third bullet point and repeat steps 3 and 4.

You can use the above steps to layer any element that's present in your slide.

Though there are transition options when moving from one slide to another, it won't matter if you don't use them.

In this section, we saw the basics to create a slide deck that won't suck. If you need a slide deck where the above design principles have been incorporated, it can be downloaded along with the bonus resources at: www.publicspeakKing.com/coast

Now, let's learn how to practice so that we can sizzle on stage.

Practice without fail

Most of the time, folks feel that their preparation is done once the deck is ready. That's a big mistake. Unless you practice, you'll not be equipped to present it well.

Here are some practice secrets that'll help you rock the presentation:

Practice in actual conditions

If you have a chance, practice in the actual conditions. This is more like the dress rehearsal before any big show. If it's going to happen in a conference room, go to the room in advance and practice in the empty room. If you are going to do a virtual presentation, join the call-through phone or Skype (even if no one joined the call), share your screen, and start speaking.

These ideas may sound silly to you but you know what—they work!

If you don't have access to actual conditions, use the power of visualization. Imagine yourself giving the presentation. Visualize the exact scenario, whether it is going to be a virtual call or an in-person presentation. Close your eyes if needed, and start practicing.

You should practice with and without the PowerPoint deck. Sometimes tech failure might happen and you might be asked to continue. Instead of saying that you cannot continue without PowerPoint, you'll impress others with your confidence to continue.

Never memorize

Have you ever forgot some content in the middle of a talk and rolled your eyes? It happened to me in third grade and it was a horrible experience. It was only years later that I understood how stupid I was. I memorized the speech, and that's why I forgot the speech after a few sentences.

What I missed was to INTERNALIZE the speech. Internalizing is the process where you drill the content, as many times as possible till you no longer have to think about the words.

How do you internalize?

Just keep saying—fast, slow, forward, backward—the content again and again. You can do this even during regular activities such as driving your car, watching television, or taking a shower. Drill the speech till the content becomes part of you. If someone wakes you up in middle of your sleep and asks you to talk about your presentation, you should talk.

We are not talking about storing it in memory. We are talking about storing it in your muscles. Your aim is to take your speech to muscle memory.

Only professionals know the following secret. Once the content is internalized, your body language, voice modulation, and confidence will improve drastically. It will have a compound effect.

Use notes

If you do not have sufficient time to commit your speech to muscle memory, you can use notes. Using notes might seem to decrease your credibility. Actually, it does not.

It is OK to use notes as long as you don't read verbatim from them.

Prepare your notes based on the overall outline of your talk. Notes can anchor your talk and help you be on track without getting lost in the depths of one particular topic.

But never assume that you can skip practice because you have notes. Even with notes you have to be comfortable with your content and that means you need to practice.

Your words must smoothly roll off your tongue.

Repeating this important point once again, there is no substitute for practice because only practice can help you present like a pro.

Present like a pro

One of the email community members of PublicSpeakKing asked me this question: "How do I know whether what I am saying is attractive to the audience?"

To answer this, I need to talk about three different types of presenters.

The first type is only concerned about themselves. They are like: "Am I going to deliver without making any mistakes?" "Am I dressed properly?" or "Is my speech attractive?" They get flustered if there are any small disturbances.

The second type is concerned about the content. They are like: "Is the listener getting what I am saying?" or "Is my message good enough for them?" They get flustered if the audience loses interest in the talk.

The third type is only concerned about making a difference in the listener's life. They are like: "How can I add more value to my audience?" or "What can they clearly implement for their own good after hearing my talk?" Whatever the situation, they'll find a way around because they genuinely care to add value to the audience.

That's exactly the mindset of a top presenter: *having a genuine care while talking to the audience.* I have seen this umpteen times. Irrespective of mistakes, nervousness, or style, the presenter who cares for the audience, wins.

Now, let us see how to handle certain specific yet common challenges that you'll face during a presentation.

How to overcome last-minute anxiety

Some scenarios can put you under a lot of pressure, such as presenting for the first time to your senior management, a multimillion-dollar make-or-break presentation, a sales presentation to a large retailer, or any other presentation that has high stakes. I have been in a few of these situations.

Even if you are not in a high-stakes presentation, you might face this situation. The following strategies work for me to tackle last-minute anxiety at a physical and psychological level. It has worked for my students at PublicSpeakKing as well. I am sure it will work for you.

Steps to tackle last-minute anxiety at a physical level:

1. Rub your left palm with your right hand for 10-15 seconds and vice versa. Do this for a few minutes till your heart rate comes to normal.

2. Slowly, breathe in and breathe out and get your heart rate to normal.

3. Sometimes, I go to a private corner where no one is around and do some vigorous punching and kicking in the air. This boosts up my energy and excitement. This has worked for me in high-pressure scenarios. I am sure a similar activity can help you too.

Steps to tackle last-minute anxiety at a psychological level:

1. Read through the following questions: What is my intent? Am I present? Will I have fun? How would I give this presentation if I knew this was the last one ever?

2. Genuinely answer the above questions. I learned them from the 2001 World Champion of Public Speaking, Darren LaCroix. The answers to the above questions will help you convert the last-minute anxiety into excitement. This is your ultimate aim. You need to get excited before taking the stage.

Handling Q&A like a pro

Many presentations in the tech world will have a question and answer session. Please don't be that guy or gal who will be happy not to get any questions from the audience. Encourage audience members to ask questions. It does not matter whether you are giving in-person or web-based presentations.

You can start off by saying, "What questions can I answer for you?" This encourages questions and is more effective and professional than saying, "Do you have any questions?"

I see many presenters do a poor job of handling questions. It just makes sense that you learn to handle this well.

- Do take a pause and answer straight to the point. Do not beat around the bush.

- Do clarify any question that is not clear. Restate the question to the questioner. This will bring clarity to you and to the audience.

- Do confirm your answer to all questions by saying, "Does that make sense?" Or "Does that answer your question?"

- Don't try to be a know-it-all but do act confident. An audience will easily figure out if you are trying to be correct when you clearly don't know the answer. If you are not sure, say that you are not sure. But if it is a genuine question, you can say confidently that you'll get back offline and provide the answer.

How to tackle glitches

During a live speech, situations could arise which were not planned. They can either fluster you or you can use them to your advantage.

The best possible way to handle problems is to be aware of the current situation. The #1 rule is *not to get flustered*. Know that your audience will empathize if there is a problem and always want you to do well. So, respect that and continue with your presentation.

I am quoting how to handle common glitches from one of my books: *The Ultimate Public Speaking Survival Guide: 37 Things You Should Know When You Start Public Speaking*.

Losing train of thought: While giving your presentation, you might lose your train of thought. It could happen because you saw someone and got distracted, or you were unsettled, or you were just anxious. If this happens, do not kick yourself.

Use the following strategy: Have some stock lines in place that can be used in case you lose your train of thought. Even if you forget, do not try to go back and share the missed portion. Here's the secret. *Remember the outline of the speech, instead of words.* If you do so, you'll know at which point of the presentation you were. Hence, you'll move on with your presentation.

Power shutting down: If power shuts down or PowerPoint does not work, just be cool as a cucumber. You can use this opportunity to say something light such as "So I will always be in the limelight" or "Was this is a plan to test my presentation skills?" If you are halfway through the presentation and power shuts down, you can say, "I think we need a break."

Once power shutdown happened during our corporate town hall. The entire power supply went off except for microphone. The speaker (our client IT head) said, "The microphone works. So, I will continue. My forehead can probably reflect the light you need." He was bald. The entire house erupted with laughter.

Cell phone ringing: This is a very common scenario. You can be prepared with an answer or two. If you feel it did not disturb the flow of your presentation, you can ignore it. If you feel it did, you can keep a few lines ready to create humor. For instance, Craig Valentine, 1999 World Champion of Public Speaking, in one of his audio programs used the following stock line: "Please tell your friend that I will call him later."

Latecomer arriving to your presentation: Someone walking in late to your presentation is a common scenario. In that case, you can choose to ignore it and act as if nothing happened. This is a good idea if the person sneaked in without disturbing the flow of your presentation. Sometimes, they might hamper the flow of your presentation. In that case, acknowledge it with a smile, or just say, "Please take a seat." The reason I am telling you to acknowledge the latecomer is to keep the attention to yourself and not let any latecomer take it away from you.

One last thing, and perhaps the most important thing when you are presenting before a live audience: Do not get caught up with the techniques. *Just focus on connecting with the audience in a genuine and authentic way.* You'll do well.

How do you keep getting better? That's where the next section will help.

Get audience feedback

Have you filled out a customer satisfaction form in a restaurant? Why do they do that? They want to know what was good, what was bad, so that they know what's working and what's not working.

Getting feedback is good. What I want to share is how to get feedback and more importantly, how to process feedback. That is the critical piece many speakers miss.

First of all, you should not bombard your audience member with a long list of questions. Just ask few simple questions such as, "If I could ask you for one thing that you liked about my presentation, what would it be?" or "Did you feel that something could be done differently?"

Now, let me share how to process feedback. If an expert gives you feedback, 99 percent of the time, the feedback will help you even if it is not what you wanted to hear. If the feedback is not from an expert, check if it makes sense. If it doesn›t, ask more people. If more people point to the same problem, you know it is time to work on it.

If you follow all the steps in this chapter, they'll help you grow as a presenter because the steps are cyclic. Every time you implement them, you'll improve your presentation skills. And please buy me a hot cup of cappuccino when you see quantifiable results.

Talking about quantifiable, what good are all the preceding chapters if we are not able to quantify our performance? And that's exactly what we'll see next.

KEY TAKEAWAYS

- Preparation is key to presentation success. Find the purpose of your presentation by interviewing the presentation planner.

- Know your audience by understanding their roles and current knowledge levels. Try to find the common experiences among them.

- Plan your structure (or outline) of the talk using SOAR or Who, What, Why, How or What, So What, Now What structure.

- Create a presentation deck by contrasting font and background, using images for complex ideas, representing table data through bar charts, and layering different elements.

- Practice in the actual conditions, internalize your presentation, and use notes if needed.

- Get excited before the presentation. Have a genuine care for the audience. Encourage the audience to ask questions. Plan for any glitches during the live presentation.

- Do not get defensive about critical feedback, but if many people give the same feedback, work on that particular feedback.

CHAPTER 7

QUANTIFYING PERFORMANCE

In which we'll see: my performance rating for the past 10 cycles, two tested ideas to create visibility, situations and approaches to get client appreciation, and two simple strategies to be more innovative

Performance is performance. It's an invaluable attitude that we need to have whether we are a newbie or a CEO. Most of the times, it's hard to quantify performance. But we shouldn't do the work throughout the year and *hope* that we get a good performance rating.

There is a famous quote by W. Edwards Deming, "In God we trust, and the rest is data." Narayana Murthy, ex-CEO of Infosys, made it famous. After hearing this quote, I used to believe that "data" meant some numbers on how quickly or how smartly I did my work, or how many people I was handling.

It's clear that I never understood data from a performance standpoint.

Data is proof to quantify our performance. This is how we can quantify: get as much visibility as possible, get as many client appreciations as possible, be innovative—in other words, document as many value-adds as possible under your name.

And we'll see each of these in detail in the rest of the chapter. Before we dig deeper, let me share my performance rating for the past 10 cycles.

My performance ratings

This might be specific to my case. The performance ratings are unique to every employer. But I want to make a point that I believe is common to any techie, or employee for that matter.

Let us look at my performance ratings over the past 10 cycles.

1 is given for a high performer, 4 for a low performer. There is a category of 1+, which is optional and given only when performance is way above the charts.

- First: 1

- Second: 1

- Third: 1+

- Fourth: 2 (Performance dipped by two levels. I must have screwed up)

- Fifth: 2

- Sixth: 2

- Seventh: 3 (Performance dipped even further. I must have really screwed up big-time)

- Eighth: 2

- Ninth: 1

- Tenth: 1

I kind of super simplified a lot of things that happened over a decade. But, I want your attention on some facts.

- My owners were different at client location and the employer base location.

- Before the performance ratings were published for the fourth cycle, I went to work at a client location at Hartford, Connecticut. My owners changed.

- Before the performance ratings were published for the seventh cycle, I traveled back from the client location. My owners changed.

A couple of questions to ask:

- If performance went down during the fourth cycle, why would I be sent to work directly with the client?

- And how come I got a performance rating of 3 during the seventh cycle, after I left client location?

Okay, Rama, get over it.

Isn't it interesting that my performance rating went down whenever my owners changed? Should I conclude that I was given a low performance rating because my owners knew that I was no longer useful to them?

I don't know if I can say that for sure. Maybe I really screwed up.

But I can say the following for sure.

Your chances of getting a better performance rating will increase only when you really perform well and make sure that your owners believe that you are going to be useful to them in future.

I know. I know. You might want to ask, "Rama, why did you continue with the company when you got a poor performance rating of 3. As in, why didn't you quit?"

Good question. Had the title not been *Confessions of a...* I would not have answered.

Well, the reason was, I was seeing someone in my floor. Hey, it's not just performance, romance is important too! And I was in the execution phase of attracting her into my life (we'll see how in Chapter 10), rather than take the traditional *arranged* marriage route.

If you don't know about arranged marriage, it's a concept where parents do all the selling so that their kids get married. They directly make the sale. No need for pickup, dating, or live-in, everything is managed end to end by parents. Isn't it sweet?

Ok, let's not lose focus on performance. The first thing is to create visibility.

How to create visibility

I was the silent hero for my first eight years. I believed that my job was to maintain peace and harmony without anybody knowing the problems that I faced.

This philosophy worked as long as my boss was directly overseeing my work. But, the silent hero became a useless hero when my boss was not overseeing my work. Nobody cared for the quality of my work. And that's how I understood why visibility matters.

Everybody wants visibility, but only a few get it, for the right reasons. Remember, we talked about perception. Creating visibility is an offshoot of the same.

Here's the game plan to be visible, at least with your boss: Be upfront with your boss that you are performance driven; keep your stakeholders in all the communications, whether emails, calls, or presentations; and never underplay your work.

And the following are tested strategies that work.

Work on critical projects

There are a lot of projects happening in an organization. Do you think it's possible that higher management will know each and every project? It's impossible. They only track critical projects.

Like an idiot, I used to say it out loud, "Oh, I won't work in that screwed-up project." I felt good about saying this. And you know what? I was so naive and wrong.

I thought life would become hard, working in such projects. What I did realize later was that it is easy to quantify performance in a critical project and it is hard to quantify performance in a stable project.

And folks who did okay in critical projects got better ratings. And my managers told me, "Rama. There is nothing special about your contribution. It is pretty much expected. You worked on pretty straightforward projects."

Working on critical projects is not always in your hand, but the next strategy is.

Be the one who runs the show

Who gets the maximum credit for a film's success? There is always a wide debate about this, but in most cases, it is the director who runs the show, and hence the director gets the credit for the film.

Your superiors will easily know whether you are playing the role of the actor or the director. The sooner you get into the director's role, the easier it is for you prove your mettle. Again, if you are new, it might not be easy. But, having this mindset helps in the long run.

There are two important traits you need to follow when you want to run the show.

Taking bottom-line responsibility:

What it means is that you'll take the responsibility without giving any excuse. You'll make sure that things get done. This is the one surefire way to show your performance.

It's not easy and you'll face a lot of challenges. Chances are many will not do this and that's your opportunity. The rewards are great because when you run the show, you can set the rules for work.

Being on top of things:

What this means is that you don't expect or assume things to happen on their own. You need to *make sure* that everything is going to happen as expected.

For example, when you commit to a deadline or delivery, you make sure that you are closely watching your team for being on track. When someone else commits on a deadline or delivery, you make sure that they are going to keep their commitment.

When I was working as scrum master for a critical project, I used to track each and every minute detail. I literally ran the show for the entire project and made my manager's job a cakewalk.

My program manager (also our client) was impressed and she sent me multiple appreciations highlighting my work. We'll talk about appreciations in the next section but appreciations will come when *you run the show and let the world know that you are running it.*

I'll never forget what she said when I needed a client approval (her approval) on a business value-add that we were proposing from a vendor perspective.

She said, "You have me in your back pocket. Send it over, and you'll have it." That's the power of running the show.

How to get appreciation

Not every techie will get a chance to directly work with a client, whether the project is product-based or service-based. But if you have a chance, you should make full use of the opportunity.

Client appreciation is like currency for your performance. And when you have client appreciations, you get appreciations from your boss as well.

Hence, the more client appreciations you have, the chance of you getting better performance ratings increases, which in turn increases chances for more money—in the form of a salary raise—in the bank.

Sometimes clients don't write appreciations but if you know that the client is happy with your work, you can very well ask for one in the disguise of a feedback. Though it sounds like a super simple plan, I never used to do this in the first eight years of my career. And this is a deep regret.

Even if you are not sure that the client is happy with your work, asking for feedback is one of the key strategies to test the waters. Just send a simple email. I've personally used the following script:

> Hi Jim,
>
> I would like to know your feedback for my work in the past six months. This will help for my performance goals.
>
> Thanks for your time.
>
> Regards
> Rama

This is one of the cornerstone principles of the start-up world. They launch an MVP (minimal viable product) and improve the product based on customer feedback. In this case, the only difference is that *you* are the product.

Once I realized the power of asking for feedback, I never stopped asking for it. Nobody does this in general, and that's why you should do it. A caveat: not everyone will give a written feedback, but that's okay. It's a numbers game. I'll explain the numbers game in the last chapter. However, the short version is: Ask every stakeholder for feedback, you'll get desired replies from a few.

If it is good, you can cash in on it for your performance rating or the next assignment. If not good, you can work on those points to improve yourself!

When you keep your boss and stakeholder happy and awe-inspired by your work, appreciations are not hard to get. Do really good work and make sure the world—clients, superiors, and stakeholders—knows that you did that work.

Here are two specific ways.

Opportunity knocks when things go wrong

When you do all things well, most of the time nobody notices it. That's the reality. Unless an issue is a pain in the neck, nobody cares. However, when things go wrong, everybody panics. And my friend, this is your opportunity. When things go wrong and you come and solve the problem, you'll be seen as a hero and you'll generate appreciation in a natural way.

I slowly started understanding that unless escalations are not directly pointed at me, they are opportunities to create visibility among my stakeholders. The farther the problem is from your area of responsibility, the greater the opportunity for you to make your mark. You don't have anything to lose. All you gain is benefit. If your solution works, you'll become a hero. If not, you'll still get a good name for trying it.

Look, I won't tell you to deliberately mess things up and then fix it. That's unethical. There won't be any difference between you and con artists.

However, what I want you to remember is, don't be the silent hero who works in the back end without anybody knowing that you took the effort to solve serious problems. Worse, don't allow any other to take that credit.

Unless the problem started because of your oversight, you have all the right to make a thing out of it. Creating a simple story arc, rather than a drum roll, will go a long way in your favor.

Create the story arc

Creating a story arc is something I discovered lately. I wish I had known how to do this earlier. I wasted many opportunities. And I don't want you to miss any opportunity going forward. This strategy is pretty exciting. Before getting into the details, let's define a good story.

A good story is where an ordinary character overcomes seemingly impossible objections to achieve a desired goal.

The above statement is the secret code behind all those movies where the hero wins at the end. The story arc is the part of the story where the obstacles increase, and it becomes seemingly impossible for the hero to overcome them.

And that's why it is the exciting part of any movie. Let's take *Godfather I* (I'm sure most of you have watched it. If not, you should).

The father (Vito Corleone) is shot and lying in a hospital bed, big brother (Sonny, who is into Mafia business) is with the family at home, rival

Mafia families have made a plan—police security removed, no other security guards—to assassinate Vito at the hospital. The hero (Michael Corleone), who happened to be visiting the hospital by chance, understands the situation.

How is the hero going to save his father? The audience watches with bated breath. And that's exactly how your stakeholders and superiors should watch you. Just that, in this case, you'll be the hero overcoming any obstacles that stand in the way to achieve the project or client goals.

Here's a case study on how I created the story arc.

Our client got non-compliance findings from a federal government audit. A multimillion-dollar project was initiated to fix the findings. I was one of the key members of that project.

The project was completed and the auditors revisited to check whether all findings were closed.

So, it was a trying time. Everything we did as part of the project was going to be questioned, and clearing the audit was a big deal for our business partners.

Business partners started asking us (techies) for a lot of data and for answers to tricky questions. I knew this was going to be tough for the next two to three weeks.

And it is at this juncture that we need to start the story arc.

So, I sent the following note to my boss because he did not know what was going on in the project.

"Fire drill is on."

I did that because I had good rapport with my boss. Even if I did not have rapport, I would have sent a note something like below.

Hi [boss]

Federal audit is happening. I am leading the back-end work. Business needs a lot of support. I might need to stretch for longer hours, for the next few weeks. Just keeping you posted.

Thanks
Rama

By sending this, I was building some panic, some excitement, and my role in the story. Again, it was not a drum roll but a subtle notification.

When the audit was over, who do you think got the visibility? Obviously, yours truly...

The appreciation from the client involved a few other team members as well. But still, I got the special visibility from my boss because I had educated him beforehand on what was going on, and what was my role.

Had I not done that, I'd just have been lost in the crowd of people who also were involved in the audit preparation and support work. When the heat is gone, people will try to be politically correct by including everyone involved in the project. And you can't blame them. So, it is your responsibility to create visibility for yourself.

Visibility gets better when appreciation emails keep moving higher and higher. Once your boss gets the client appreciation, your boss will reply all, keeping his or her boss in copy. Then, the boss above your boss will reply all, keeping his or her boss in copy. And you know, before you realize it, you have created huge visibility.

A caveat: if your boss is completely aware of your work and directly involved in overseeing you and your work, you might not need the above strategy.

Use common sense while applying the above ideas. Talking about common sense, let's use it to be more innovative.

How to be more innovative

If there is one thing almost all technology companies are talking, it's innovation.

Do you have an overwhelming thought that you should be on the cutting edge of innovation and technology? If you have the inclination to learn new technologies, you should go for it.

But, let us start with basics.

Every organization is trying to create value—that's it.

The goal of innovation is doing something that creates value. Value could be creating a bestselling product, creating a process that improves efficiency, or even creating a simple yet useful tool for your company or client.

So the question is: How do we go about innovation?

We all know the adage "Necessity is the mother of invention." If necessity is the mother of invention, then I believe problem is the mother of innovation.

The easiest way to be more innovative is to start from the pain points of the project, such as tasks taking too long or functionalities that are breaking often.

Try to simplify stuff one step at a time.

The simplest start for innovation, for software services, would be to solve problems-that-nobody-states for your customers.

When I was working at Aetna, I used to be in charge of the development team as well as the production support. If a job run failed at night, I had to get up and first respond to the production support team, "Hey, I am working on it." If I didn't do it, the page would go to my client manager at night.

And the next day, I'd be in a conference room to answer why I did not respond at night.

This whole process flow was risky more than being painful. This had been the process for several years. The folks before me did the same thing. However, there was another way.

Our team in India was available during the US night. I asked my management if the offshore team could handle production support. They were like, "Umm. I don't think senior management will approve this." And I was like, "I did not ask for a penthouse in Manhattan. It's just a pager." I left off the matter.

One day, while checking how the pager messages were routed, I stumbled upon the fact that there were two ways to contact the support. One was through pager and the other through email. Nobody bothered about email because job fail alerts had to be immediate and pager was the go-to alert mechanism. I got an idea.

I updated the offshore email IDs along with the pager alerts. I changed the process flow. I told my India team, "If you get an email alert for job fail, first call the production support group and tell them that we are working on it. Then, work on the solution. Only in urgent cases, call me up." That's it.

No more painful experience of getting up at night. No more painful experience of dreading that I'd miss the pager alert and my client manager would call up my boss. And I don't need to explain how well I slept without attending the pager.

As a first step, check the pain areas in your software application: whether any process takes a long time to run, or fails quite often. If yes, then investigate the root cause. It could be as simple as rewriting an SQL query or indexing some columns in your table. Once, by suggesting the addition of one index in one of our relational tables, a job process that used to run six hours ran in one minute.

It's not always that you need to be innovative from a technical front.

One of the recent roles I did was of a scrum master. If you are not sure, a scrum master acts as a bridge between business partners and technology teams for a project executed in agile methodology. We were planning to launch a campaign to contact customers of our client org.

We built new letter and email templates, and built functionality to trigger it as well. Application A had to send feed to application B, which would trigger physical letters or emails. The plan was to send emails to those customers who gave consent to be contacted by email. For the rest of them, we planned to trigger physical letters.

One month before the launch, we realized we had a problem. Application A assumed that application B would fetch preference and email IDs of customers. Application B assumed that application A would feed preference and email IDs for those customers for whom email needs to be triggered. So, there was a deadlock.

There was no way application A could do development work in order to get email IDs. We had a critical launch within one month. When we probed and tried to find all possible options, we found that application B had a functionality called bounce back.

What that means is if application B went ahead with the email trigger even without a valid email ID, an email to the customer would be triggered as long as the customer had updated their email ID in the client database. If the email ID was not found, there would be a bounce back, and a physical letter would get triggered.

This was perfect. We techies felt that we could leverage this. And I had to do the selling to our business partners. I proposed to business that we "default all communication to email." The only problem with this solution was that we might be contacting customers who might not have given consent in their preferences. But I convinced compliance business that this campaign was for a compliance mandate, and we didn't need customer consent on this. Business agreed.

This had many advantages: our launch went on time, we reached customers faster because there were more emails, less physical letters resulted in less cost to client, and we avoided the development cost for application A.

The other way to innovate, related to software products, is to see what is working and make it better with your own spin.

Steve Jobs copied GUI technology from Xerox. Bill Gates copied GUI technology from Apple.[1] The biggest social media website, Facebook, ripped off users from Myspace by adding more features, and creating a great user experience. The list goes on.

I really respect Steve Jobs, Bill Gates, and Mark Zuckerberg. They have used technology to change the world in their own way. I used their examples to prove a point that even *they* copied and added their own spin. In the charming book *Steal Like an Artist,* Austin Kleon says, "All creative work builds on what came before. Nothing is completely original."

We don't need to get too bogged down by some obscure technology term. And especially when your leadership or management is talking about innovation—it's a 99 percent chance that they do not know what to innovate either. Somewhere we feel that we need to do earth-shattering stuff like the next industry-best practice or operating system. And hence, most of the time, we end up not doing anything. That's the not right attitude either. You don't need to do earth-shattering things. But at least have your thought process tuned to be more innovative. That's the key.

And what's coming next is one of the simplest yet potent tools.

Ask questions

"Could you put a message at the bottom of everybody's screen?" asked Tim Draper, the famous venture capitalist. As Adam Penenberg describes the meeting in *Viral Loop,* Hotmail founders Sabeer Bhatia and Jack Smith sat across the table from Tim. They were discussing how to get the word out about Hotmail. Bhatia said, "Oh, come on, we don't want to do that!"

"But can you technically do it?... And it can persist, right? You can put it on one message, and if he sends an email to somebody else, you can put it on that one, too, right?" asked Tim.

"Yeah, yeah," Smith replied. Tim said, "So put 'P.S.: I love you. Get your free email at Hotmail' at the bottom."

And that simple idea went on to make Hotmail a household name, and six months later, they sold Hotmail for millions of dollars.

When you send emails from your smartphone, have you observed that your emails carry an additional line that says, "Sent from iPhone" or "Sent from Blackberry" or "Sent from HTC EVO 4G"? Well, this is just an extension of the above idea, which has become an industry standard to market products.

Can you see how questions can lead to innovation? If we have access to clients of software application (business application), we need to ask:

- Why are we working on [something]? (Replace [something] with whatever you are working on.)

- Is the client benefitting by following the current approach?

- Is there an easier way to do the same thing?

If we have access to the end users of a software application (product), we need to ask:

- What will make their life better?

- What features will be useful for them?

- Are we focusing our time and energy on things that create maximum value for clients?

Innovation can stem from asking questions. While questions are one approach to innovation, applying what you observe is another approach.

Apply what you observe

Terms such as lateral thinking or thinking outside the box have become fads. Here's the thing. If you can apply a concept you learned outside your work in your work, you'll foster innovation.

The most classic example is how Isaac Newton's observation of an apple falling from a tree inspired him to deduce the law of gravity.

Now that might be a far-fetched example but the following one is not.

Robert Kearns invented intermittent windshield wipers based on how our eyes function.[2] Our eyes blink only for a few seconds rather than continuously. One day when driving in rain, he was irritated by the continuous movement of his windshield wipers. Suddenly, he realized, why not create a wiper that functions like the human eye, which blinks intermittently?

You never know how you'll find solutions. Not just at work, from anywhere in your life, there might be solutions in disguise. Innovation does not mean creating new letters of a language. It could just mean creating new words from the letters of a known language. Or it could even mean creating new sentences of a known language.

Along with innovation, there is a lot of emphasis on automation through tools. Automation adds value when we reduce any effort that is manual and repeated regularly. What we create through automation should be useful.

I also see that for the sake of creating, folks create tools that nobody uses. There was one guy in my team who kept creating tools time and again. I asked him, "Does our team even know that you are creating these tools?" He said, "I am not sure."

I did not want to be rude to him because he was at least doing something. I told him, "Whenever you create a tool, give a quick demo session to the entire team. Ask them to give feedback. Based on their feedback, improve on the tool to create something useful for the team."

Any automation or automation tool that nobody uses is not a value-add. You need to first influence people to buy your ideas. And they'll buy your ideas if what you offer them is useful. Only when people are using our tools, we can call it a value-add, which is the ultimate goal of innovation.

We took a look at quantifying performance, but what good is it if we don't know how to handle the hard stuff that comes our way at work?

You guessed it right. That's what we will cover next.

KEY TAKEAWAYS

- Your chances of getting a better performance rating will increase only when you perform well and make sure that your owners believe that you are going to be useful to them in future.

- Create visibility by being the director, and not just an actor. Be on top of things and take bottom-line responsibility. Always work on critical projects, not mediocre projects.

- Client appreciation is like currency for your performance. Use feedback and story arc to manufacture appreciations.

- Innovation and automation are just means. What we need to focus on is creating value.

CHAPTER 8

HOW TO HANDLE THE HARD STUFF

In which we'll learn about: handling change of owner, must-haves before asking for a raise, what was discovered in the longest study on adult life, creating job security, saying NO to false urgencies and much more

Technology companies—especially the big ones—are the pioneers in creating office campuses that can compete with resorts and luxury hotels. They have everything: tennis courts, high-end food courts and cafes, swimming pools, squash courts, and salons.

Even small startups may offer a fancy work environment. If we are not careful, we might feel like we are in la-la land, but the fact is that the employer owns you for the stipulated 40 hours per week.

We should not wake up one day and think, "Oh my gosh. This is not what I thought it was," because of some of the hard stuff that comes our way including change of owner, asking for a raise or promotion, facing escalations, concerns about job security and safety, and negative emotions.

Change of owner

I started my career in Pune (India), a city 740 miles away from my hometown. After working for three years, I wanted to take a transfer to my hometown. But, I was not sure.

So I took my previous manager for a coffee. We went to the cafeteria and I mentioned my aspirations for transfer. Without missing a beat, he said, "You will face ownership issues. People won't take your ownership." What he meant was, "You will not get a good performance rating." It became clear that if I took a transfer, it would be a bad move.

One of my colleagues took a transfer because she was getting married. You know what performance rating she got? Four—the worst performance rating. I know she is not a bad performer. I also know that if she had been in the original location, she would have got a better rating.

You might feel "owner" is a harsh word. Well, it is harsh because the word "owner" reminds us of the word "slave." I'll be the first one to say that you never need to be a "slave." Again, there are shitty work environments. If you are in such an environment, just get the heck out of there.

But a change of ownership will impact you even in companies with strong values and cultures. Hence, you need to be clear and careful on the impact of ownership change. At the onset, you will feel that your boss is your owner. But, that is not entirely true. There will be leadership levels above your boss.

You might not report to them directly but you need to know the line of leadership. It'll be helpful in situations where your boss changes—transferred, quit, or fired—and you get a new boss. And that's why it is always good to maintain all aspirations and appreciations documented in emails. This is one specific scenario where the documented emails will save you and your aspirations.

I can't emphasize enough on documenting things in email.

Coming to our change, since owners discourage change, how can we handle change in a way that it won't impact us adversely?

Start discussing your movement after your performance ratings are handed out to you.

If you reveal your intentions of moving earlier, you might end up... well, you know. You might say this is not fair. Who said performance ratings are fair? There are exceptions, but rarely will any owner help once they feel that you are no longer useful.

Raise or promotion

Bosses act funny. If they want to give you a promotion or raise, they'll find a way. If they don't want to give you a promotion or raise, they will still find a way not to give it. Sometimes I feel that employers behave like my dad. Both pre-decide what they want and then change the policy accordingly.

All properly managed companies give promotions or raises based on performance. If you have the best performance ratings, your chance of negotiating a raise or promotion is high, though it is not guaranteed.

If you don't have performance-related data points, your chance of negotiating a raise or promotion is low. But that does not mean you should not ask.

The one who does not ask, does not get anything, be it a promotion or a salary hike. Only when you have this uncomfortable conversation will you know the true picture. They'll tell you the specific items that they are looking for in order to give you a raise or promotion.

Let us say that you improved your performance over the past few years and have a strong case for a promotion. Do you just keep waiting and hope that your boss and HR will talk to each other about you and give you a promotion?

No way.

You should go and have a discussion. If you have the data, most probably, they'll ask you to wait for a few more months. Here's where you should be respectful and agree with them. But document the conversation by sending out an email to your boss or HR on time frame and promise. This is just to document the discussion because you never know when your boss or HR or both might change.

What you shouldn't do is show arrogance in a way that says, "If you don't give me a promotion, I'll quit my job." That's arrogant and stupid. Chances are they will get offended and find a replacement for you. Things run based on trust. If trust is gone, then it will become hard for everyone. But if you don't trust your management, it might be a good idea to search for other job offers and have a few of them ready.

After a few months, most probably, your raise or promotion might have not gone through. You again go and discuss your raise or promotion. You say to your bosses, "Well, I was hoping to see my promotion go through."

Boss: "Things are pretty tight. Let's see in the next cycle." (Clearly, it's not working.)

You: "OK, in that case I might need to pursue different options. X Company has offered me that role."

Boss: "Oh, OK, let me talk to my boss and get back." Or your boss might say, "OK, that's great news. When is your start date?" (So you better be prepared if your company is ready to let you go.)

Here's my own experience negotiating for a promotion. A few years ago, when the promotion cycle happened, I did not get promoted. Folks at my experience level got promoted. I asked my manager about this. He had no clue, so I went to his boss who said, "Oh, I did not know that you were expecting a promotion." I was like, "Really."

I had a heated discussion with my boss and his boss on this.

That's when I realized nobody bothers about you. Unless you go and state your intentions clearly, you are not going to get anything.

And in the next cycle, I got the promotion. I would bet a thousand bucks that I would not have got that promotion in the next cycle, had I not had that heated debate when I did not get the promotion.

The following is so critical that it's worth repeating.

Have relevant data points

If you got married or took out a mortgage, you might need more money, but your company does not care. They will only care if you add value to the project or the company. Your intention when negotiating for a raise or salary should be based on your performance and value added to the organization.

It's the only way you might win. If there is a proper performance rating and your company determines promotion only based on that, then ratings are enough. If they are expecting any other value-adds, then have documented proofs of value-add.

Having an offer at hand

Having an offer can be the best thing, but don't use it to threaten your current company overtly. It's a proper proof that you are worth much more than your current salary or position. In fact, your offer will help your boss reach out to his or her boss or talk to HR about your situation. After all, your boss also needs data points to make a case for your raise or promotion.

But if things don't work out, you can always make the move without spoiling your image at the current job. Since, you never know if you'd like to come back to your current job.

One of the side effects (or rather, straight effect) of not getting a raise or promotion is you become *emotional*. Let's talk about becoming emotional at work.

Becoming emotional

Early in my career, my team lead told me, "Keep your emotions out of your work."

But how can we keep emotion out of work? Tony Robbins, arguably the leading authority in self-development and motivation, said that *emotion* is the drive for human action in his famous TED talk[1] "Why we do what we do."

During my assignment at Aetna, I was responsible for a critical project. The project had high visibility. A number of critical features, applications, and teams were involved. There was a problem. The architect of the project sucked. The project manager sucked. When the project went live, lots of issues cropped up, and the blame game started. The project manager blamed the tech team because he did not have the balls to question the architect.

Since my business partner was paying for the project, full pressure fell on me to resolve issues. Though I was supporting the project with my full strength, I was asked to take ownership for the defects. I refused do so. Animosity was just flying in the air. Emotional outbursts happened. Ego clashes started and it was pure chaos.

At the end of the day, I did not get any benefit from that whole episode. For the pain it caused, I felt it was not worth it. And I think my team lead was right when she said to keep emotions out of work.

Once my friend told me that a techie jumped from the top of a building inside the office campus and took his own life. Why would that person take such a drastic step?

People take such drastic steps when they do not have emotional support. I worked as a helpline volunteer for a suicide-prevention NGO, which provided emotional support to people with suicidal tendencies. My job was to answer phone calls. All kinds of people—rich, middle class, poor—called for emotional support. They had one thing in common. They were emotionally down. Being emotionally down is not good for a techie because it sucks the enthusiasm out of the workplace.

Observe your emotions right now. Are you complaining that your manager is micromanaging you? Are you not happy with the company policy? Are you picking a fight with family members for no good reason? Chances are that you are emotionally charged up.

"Anyone can become angry—that is easy. But to be angry with the right person, to the right degree, at the right time, for the right purpose, and in the right way—this is not easy," said Aristotle in *Nicomachean Ethics*.

On the other hand, are you not talking with anyone around you? Do you come in, log in to your desk, do the assigned work for the sake of it and leave? Are you not feeling like talking to your peers or friends? Chances are that you are emotionally down.

These scenarios are at the extreme ends of a scale. Most of the time, we are leaning towards one end or the other. However, our aim should be to move towards the center of the scale. We need to balance our emotions. In next chapter, we'll discuss four ways to reduce our stress, which in turn will balance our emotions.

Here's the thing. It's not practical for folks at work to solve your emotional issues. Chances are they don't know or don't want to know your needs. That's why it's really important to have healthy and strong relationships with your immediate family and friends. The sad reality is people are spending more time having a truckload of virtual friends instead of nurturing those few relationships that can provide emotional support.

Isn't it interesting that we let go of a lot of great friends just because we moved on in life?

I confess, even I am guilty of this. We just don't take the time and effort to maintain the relationship. I don't think we need to keep sending expensive gifts. A simple check-in email or text such as "Hello, how are you?" will mean a lot to them. I tried implementing this lately and trust me, I felt really good doing this simple exercise.

What I am going to share now might be the essence of what every human needs to know. In one of the most viewed TED talks, "What makes a good life? Lessons from the longest study on happiness," Robert Waldinger said:

> The Harvard Study of Adult Development may be the longest study of adult life that's ever been done. For 75 years, we've tracked the lives of 724 men, year after year, asking about their work, their home lives, their health, and of course asking all along the way without knowing how their life stories were going to turn out. Studies like this are exceedingly rare. Almost all projects of this kind fall apart within a decade because too many people drop out of the study, or funding for the research dries up, or the researchers get distracted, or they die, and nobody moves the ball further down the field. But through a combination of luck and the persistence of several generations of researchers, this study has survived. About 60 of our original 724 men are still alive, still participating in the study, most of them in their 90s. And we are now beginning to study the more than 2,000 children of these men. And I'm the fourth director of the study.

Then Robert got into more details and concluded: "So what have we learned? What are the lessons that come from the tens of thousands of pages of information that we've generated on these lives? Well, the lessons aren't about wealth or fame or working harder and harder. The clearest message that we get from this 75-year study is this: Good relationships keep us happier and healthier. Period."[2]

Though we need to nurture all the relationships, we'll focus on one key relationship—our romantic relationships—in Chapter 10. That's absolutely critical, as we usually seem to learn about it the hard way.

Talking about hard, what could be harder than fear of escalations?

Fear of escalations

If there is one word to scare a techie, it is "escalation." When I started my career, I used to be a fearful kid thinking, "I hope this does not get escalated to my boss."

If appreciations are the elixir, escalations are the toxin. When escalations happen, people panic like a deer in the headlights because it's a high-pressure scenario. Sometimes, things get messed up because of your miss. If you are the type of person who takes your job seriously, you shouldn't break down if an escalation happens against you.

Maybe, you really messed up. So what? Things happen.

Your ideal mindset should be "Failure is not an option." But on top of that, if there is a miss, we just can't sit down and cry. Hey, we are not driving a plane. What is the worst that can happen? They might ask you to leave the job. That does not mean your life is over. It's a level playing field out there. You can find ways to make money for paying bills till you get another lucrative job.

One way to bulletproof your fear is to start working on creating passive income right away, so that you don't feel the pressure of job insecurity or escalations. We'll cover passive income in the chapter about money.

Back to handling escalations, when they happen, everybody from your boss to his or her boss, customers, and stakeholders, will be watching you.

First things first: Address the problem at hand instead of pushing the blame to others. Then, stay calm and composed instead of panicking.

All the stakeholders usually panic. Being a techie, you must give them the confidence that things will be okay and work with your team to resolve the issue as soon as possible.

Looking back, the specifics of the escalation won't matter. What will matter is how you handled the pressure. What perception you created among your company leaders. That's what matters.

In the midst of being true to yourself and the company, never ever take chances on safety and security.

Personal safety and security breaches

Most companies have good safety policies. But untoward incidents happen even in these glorified campuses. If there is a situation that requires you to work alone or in weird hours, and you feel unsafe, you better take caution. Don't risk your safety. It's not worth it.

Raise the issue with your stakeholder and push the work to the next working day. No work is more important than your safety and that of your colleagues. Don't put them in an unsafe position. Point out potential problems to them.

The other aspect of safety is data security. Do not attempt any task that can jeopardize your integrity or your company's integrity. Data security breaches are taken very seriously. I have seen people lose their jobs because of security breaches.

Let us say that you have a key project deadline coming up in a few days. You need access to a client server, which can be accessed only by your colleague, who is on leave for the next few days. Instead of finding a person who can access the server, or calling your colleague to log in remotely, you access the server using your colleague's credentials. If the client team tracks this activity and initiates an inquiry, you'll be in the soup.

Let us take another scenario. You are working on a project, which has only a one-month timeline. The requirements document came late and you need to move as fast as possible on this. You forward the requirements document to your personal ID so that you can read it at home during the weekend. Next day, HR emails you asking for an explanation. You say, "It was for the project goals."

HR says, "You breached basic security protocols. We need to terminate your assignment." Though the intentions were good, was this worth it? Nope.

Instead of putting yourself or your job at stake, find alternatives. If you are asked to work odd hours or weekends, request work-from-home options and do a remote login.

If a deadline is fast approaching, seek to talk with the client and explain the possible delays. When in doubt, as I said before, *discuss and align with your stakeholder*. This simple strategy will always save you, and ensure your job security.

Is there a way that we can create job security? Let's see that next.

Creating job security

Once upon a time, when you filed a health insurance claim, the following happened. Your application was filed manually through a letter. Then the details were checked from one department to another. Finally, a person manually approved—maybe used an ink pen to sign—a document telling whether the company could approve this claim.

Currently, every step of the process is automated using technology. Without any manual intervention, the claim gets approved, and the customer even gets the notification in email or as a text message.

Long ago, people went to banks to withdraw money. Then ATMs cropped up. A person just walks across the street to plug in the card, gets the cash, and gets a receipt of the balance.

Almost every major business has transformed its process by using technology, and software techies played a major role in this transformation.

Were there job losses during this transformation? Of course there were but things evolved.

First businesses used technology to refine and shape their process at the enterprise level. Then they focused on optimizing their operations. Then came the need for businesses to make intelligent systems to make decisions. This resulted in a new field of business intelligence. They collected entire enterprise data, and queried to find insights for making business decisions. Now, businesses are looking to build systems and advanced analytics using historical and real-time unstructured data, thus ushering us into the big data era.

There is also a lot of talk about IT budgets being cut year after year. The bad news is it is true. But, the good news is that there are investments in newer trends and technologies.

Businesses want to predict customer trends and behaviors so that they can tailor their products and services. And companies at the forefront of using these latest technologies are making it big.

How do you think Amazon knows what kind of products you might need and suggests exactly the same? Do you know that whatever you are buying is tracked? Do you know the number of times you take a service is tracked?

How about the business of social media? You may think that Facebook is a social media company helping you connect with friends and have fun. Really? Facebook is fundamentally an advertising company. That's how Mark Zuckerberg makes money. Facebook owns your data and sells it to other businesses. Whether you know it or not, Facebook knows everything. Not just know; they track all the information: when you changed your status from engaged to married, when you changed your job title, which ad you clicked, which website you visited from Facebook, which blog post you read, and a million other things. They are a data-driven company. Based on this data, other businesses can advertise to you.

Let us say a wedding photographer wants to find new leads. He can advertise to people in New York or New Delhi who changed their status to "engaged" last month.

Let us say you want to sell designer shoes for women. You can exactly target women under 30 (not that older women don't like fancy shoes) working in corporate jobs. The range of options that Facebook gives you to target the demographic is mind-blowing.

I can give you more examples but I think you understood how advanced technology is disrupting the way business is done. It's the reality we are in. Advanced technology is changing businesses. There is a reason I am using the word "advanced" because traditional databases and applications (they only handle structured data) do not cut it here.

Product tech companies such as Amazon, Facebook, and Google are disrupting how business is done using advanced technologies. There is no denying that all major businesses want to leverage this shift for their growth.

And techies are the workforces to bring in this disruption. Technologies get changed, but not people. You'll be ahead as long as you are ready to re-skill yourself in the latest opportunities. Learn agile methodologies, learn advanced skills for UX and UI, learn big data technologies and associated areas such as JavaScript, Hadoop, Scala, Spark, machine learning, Python, or anything that is current in the marketplace. If you are good with math and statistics, aspire to become a data scientist.

You'll be amazed that big data-related technologies are open source. Companies like Hortonworks and Cloudera give free infrastructure (non-commercial licenses) needed to perform hands-on. There is a ton of material available. Check out Coursera, w3schools, or your company knowledge management repository.

You know your current skillset. See which latest skill will add logical value to your overall skillset. And get good at it in your spare time. If you don't have opportunities, at least be ready by passing industry-recognized certifications.

You'll never have to worry about jobs going away because you'll be ready for the current job demands. I'll sum it up with the beautiful statement written by Robert Greene in *Mastery*. "The future belongs to those who learn more skills and combine them in creative ways. And the process of learning skills, no matter how virtual, remains the same."

False urgency

False urgency means creating unnecessary pressure by asking us to stretch or go out of the way when there is no real need.

Some managers make a big deal out of every internal deadline. Your boss might ask you to stay late or work on a weekend when there is no delivery planned for next week.

I am not telling you to leave work at a critical juncture. There can and usually will be exceptional situations when you need to work longer hours or during weekends. Even that should be tracked so that you can use them to showcase your performance.

But don't get offended when your boss asks you to complete that stupid false-urgency task when you are ready to leave for the day. Just ask a simple question, "Is this really that important that it cannot wait till tomorrow?"

If your boss is sensible, there will be no issues. If not, you'll have to think again about working under such a boss.

The root cause of false urgency is improper estimations to complete a task. This is a big problem in the tech world. So many projects get screwed up because of *improper estimates*. Hence, you need to be careful about committing to impossible schedules. That means you need to be careful when committing to a deadline. Say someone asks you, "Hey, can you finish this by tomorrow?" Unless you are confident about the task, don't say YES or NO. Just say, "I'll start off with it on priority."

A straightforward activity like applying a set of rules is easy to estimate. But, activity that is not so straightforward—changing requirements, design, architecture, algorithm and solution discussion—is not easy to estimate.

These tasks take time to mature because most of the time, no one person has all the inputs. Whenever you are asked to give an ETA, add a healthy buffer and use the word "tentative."

For example, if you know that a task can be completed in eight business days, you'll say, "We are working on it. I'll keep you updated on the progress. The tentative end date could be few weeks from now." A few weeks translates to 10 business days and you have used "tentative" to protect yourself from uncontrollable impediments such as hard to get DBA's time, hard to get architect's time, a long weekend coming up, or any other blockage.

The impediments could vary based on your situation but *adding a buffer and keeping the deadline tentative* will always protect you from false urgency.

You might have realized that I am arguing that performance is the only thing that matters at work. But here's the harsh reality. Your performance at work matters only for your employer. There is something bigger, which is performance in life.

And it is our responsibility. Always keep asking whether what you are working is also making sense to your life. Is it helping you get what you want from life?

We should not sacrifice our time with our loved ones because of false urgencies. We should not sacrifice our health because of false urgencies. And finally, we definitely should not pass our golden years without creating financial freedom and meaning for our life.

And that's why I want to cover health, romantic relationships, money, and unleashing our potential in the next part.

KEY TAKEAWAYS

- Document all aspirations in email. Make your move for change after you get your performance rating.

- Always have data points when asking for a raise or promotion. Have an offer at hand while negotiating a raise or promotion.

- Keep emotions out of your work. Strengthen your relationship with your loved ones for getting emotional support.

- During escalations, we need to solve the issue at hand but remain calm and composed.

- No work is worth the risk of personal safety. Your job is not safe if you breach data security policies.

- Technology is not going away—it's changing rapidly. Your job is secure as long as you are willing to re-skill in newer technologies and modern methodologies.

- Do not entertain false urgency. Ask, "Is this really needed today, or can it wait till the next day?"

- More than work, it is in life that we need to really perform.

PART 2

The things that matter in Personal life

CHAPTER 9

HACKING OUR WAY TO A HEALTHY LIFE

In which we'll learn about: power of keystone habits; simple hacks for eating right, handling negativity and complaints; and four tested strategies to handle stress

When we talk about an army guy, what come to our mind? Naturally, we think about descriptions such as fit and healthy. For some reason, we don't associate these descriptions with techies.

Health and techies just don't seem to be associated. Is it because we sit in comfortable chairs within colorful cubicles, in air-conditioned spaces, sipping lattes?

The thing is we all know what is right for our life and health. It's just that we seem to be messed up with the lifestyle, which is dictated by the patterns that we are accustomed to. We need to break the pattern that is governing us.

That's why we need to hack our way to a healthy life. And to do that, I want to talk about something that is really powerful. In fact, I started believing in this concept so much that I have taken it as my personal agenda to practice and recommend to others.

I'll be the first one to say that sometimes I fail to apply this concept in all areas of my life. But I have seen tremendous results when I do apply it to certain areas of my life.

I am talking about the power of habits.

The power of habits

Habits are the programs of our body. Habits create AUTOMATION. Yes, automating our brain and body. It is much larger than willpower, or intention, which are... still manual. So, they are prone to error. Who else can understand automation better than techies!

Whether you know it or not, there is automation built inside you. As soon as you enter the room, your fingers switch on the fan or light whether power is on or off. You just can't help it. The moment you go near the switch, your hand goes to that switch even though power might be off.

For example, if you learn a new technology or language for an hour every day, you'll be able to clear a top certification within just three months.

If you spend time on a treadmill for 20 minutes per day for one year, your body transformation will happen.

If every day you skip breakfast, have a late lunch, and sleep only for four hours, you'll end up looking four years older after one year!

That's the power of habit.

There is a scientific reason for this. In the phenomenal book *The Power of Habit,* Charles Duhigg reported that our habits are stored in the basal ganglia, an area of the brain associated with involuntary actions.

Think about it. Your habits go and hang out with involuntary actions like applying a sudden brake or bouncing back your hand when you touch a hot cup. Those are involuntary; your body automatically knows what to do.

How cool would it be to use habits to hack doing things you know are good for you but you don't do? Such as exercising every morning, eating fresh veggies, avoiding long hours of watching TV, or hanging out with supportive friends?

Consciously form habits that are aligned with your goals and then let those habits hang out with these involuntary actions. This is like automating those manual tasks. You are a techie—you got this.

Look, it is not a straightforward thing to form habits. There will be obstacles. The main obstacle is starting. That's why it is highly recommended that you start with something really small.

I'll explain more on how to tackle the obstacles and cement habits in next section but before that I want you to leverage a powerful concept called *keystone habits*.

Keystone habits are the key

Keystone habits are activities that create a chain reaction to change your other habits in a massive way. These are mini habits that have the power to change how you do all other things.

Let's use exercise as an example. I'm not talking about going to the gym or building a lean body. I'm just talking about simple 10- to 15-minute exercise.

I'll take my own example. I am not overweight. I always was mindful about my eating habits but not about exercising. It was because I thought simple exercising was not helping me build muscles or tone my body. So, why should I waste time on such activities? Makes sense, right? No, I was wrong.

Let me explain. The mere act of a doing few simple exercises in the morning will kick in keystone habits, which will give an advantage.

Let's assume that we created a 10-minute exercise. Just 10 minutes—nothing more, nothing less. Sounds easy (sometimes, that's exactly why many won't do it). Since you have decided to do a 10-minute exercise, you'll get up before 7 a.m. (depending on your work schedule, of course). Maybe 6:45 a.m. Common, that's not bad. I am not asking for 5 a.m. or 6 a.m.

Because you need to get up at 6:45 a.m., you'll start looking at going to bed a little early. For an eight-hour sleep, you'll have to be asleep before 11 p.m.

Now, after exercise, you are out of the zombie zone. You are sharp by 7 a.m. so that you can exchange morning greetings with your near and dear ones, or read a book or do something that's useful for your long-term goals.

Since you have been burning your calories since 7 a.m., your body will automatically ask you for food. You can have a proper breakfast at home or office by 9 a.m.

You'll reach the office early.

Because you got in early and no one else was around, you finish most of your tasks productively (come on, you and I know that *people disturbing you* is the #1 productivity sucker).

Because you finished your tasks early, you have time to focus on fresh ideas for improving any aspect of the work or project.

Because you ate breakfast by 9 a.m., you'll feel hungry by 1 p.m. and have lunch. Again focus back on work, and leave the office on time. When you have time for yourself after work, you can play with pals, go on a date, or join your family to spend the evening with them.

Since you had lunch on time, you will feel hungry by 7 or 8 p.m. and have dinner. And because your body did so many things throughout the day, it starts getting shut down by 11 p.m. You get up the next day at 6:45 a.m. and the cycle continues.

Look at the crazy benefits it can provide:

- You are eating at proper times.

- You are becoming more productive at the office.

- You are spending quality time with friends and family.

- You have time to work on your long-term goals.

And I did not even talk about the health benefits of doing the exercise!

Just the very act of getting up and showing up for exercise at a stipulated time can have a profound impact on your life. I'll be the first to admit that it is easy to skip such a simple thing as doing exercise for 10 minutes a day in the morning.

You might ask, "How can I control my urge to skip the habit routine?" I found the secret to form and cement a habit when I read *The One Thing* by Gary Keller. The secret is to be *disciplined enough* till the habits take over. Disciplined just enough to hold on with the activity till it becomes a habit. Discipline is like the rocket, and habit is like the satellite.

For example, let us say you want to cultivate the exercise habit at 6:45 a.m. You might exercise for a week, but you might want to miss a day because of travel or flu or any unplanned event. In that case, just try doing one simple exercise, which might take just 10 or 15 seconds. You don't need a venue or motivation to do this. You just need to *do it* so that the discipline is alive. There is power in showing up every day. Essentially, you are just disciplining your mind. And thus, by keeping at it, in a matter of time, the habit routine will take over.

So the question is, "What do you want to work on and get good at, so that habits can kick in and do magic?"

Think about it. This is powerful stuff. Nobody talks about such things in day-to-day conversations. And yet it is those simple day-to-day activities that help you do larger things. I am here to tell you these things work. I am writing my sixth book, and habits are the real secret to get things going on autopilot.

However, habits work both ways. If we are not mindful, habits can harm as well. And that's why we need to be very mindful about what we are eating, which is what we'll see next.

Mind your food

Techies are the best consumers. To refresh ourselves, we drink Coca-Cola or Pepsi-Cola. The sugar in them makes us fat, so we decide to get a gym membership to burn them off.

We consume burgers, donuts, lattes, coffees, pizzas in such huge quantities that multiple industries would run out of business if we stop consuming them. It's not that you or I don't know that it is bad for health, but we do it anyway because it is easily available.

We wouldn't fill our car tank with sub-par gasoline just because it smells good or it's clean. We want fuel that gives maximum efficiency and won't harm the engine. I sometimes wonder, then why would we consume stuff that's neither good for the body nor gives us maximum efficiency?

If we spend our money on processed food (which is mostly junk), we can get out of shape and then we enroll in gyms, pay for nutrition pills and supplements, or even medicine and hospital bills. Did you see how many industries are involved here?

Do you really think that the government will ban food that's bad for our health?

I started putting on the dangerous flab once I hit 28. I hated it. So, I went about researching diet and health. I am only a techie, not a doctor or a nutritionist. Here's what I found:

- The tummy or extra flab is not because of intake of fat, as I had believed. The extra carbs from your regular food get converted into fat because they are more than you need for your day-to-day activities.

- Sugars, grains, and dairy form the basis of our staple diet, but they are carbohydrates and overconsumption of them leads to excess flab.

- You reduce your flab not only by skipping the bad stuff, but by eating the good stuff as well.

- A fit body is not necessarily a healthy body. Keeping your body healthy is around 80 percent nutrition and 20 percent fitness. That's why it is very important to mind the quality of the ingredients. *Always go for quality of food versus quantity of food.*

Look, I am going to oversimplify and help you understand a little about basic nutrition. There are some basic nutrients that the body needs: carbohydrates, calcium, proteins, fats, vitamins, minerals, fiber, and water.

I don't want to advocate on what type of diet—vegan, vegetarian, or non-vegetarian— to follow. But I want to say that you should put nutrients into your body whether you follow a vegan, vegetarian, or non-vegetarian diet or you take a good quality supplement.

So, what's the stuff that you shouldn't put into your body?

Anything that is *fried, processed, and prepackaged* is bad for your flab, and for your overall health. If you can just avoid these foodstuffs, your body will thank you many times.

Unless you are very seriously looking to become a supermodel, you can work around few things.

- Eat homemade food. Being a techie, you ask, where do I have the time? If that's true, something is really wrong with the way you are working. If you are in India, it might be a wise idea to invest in a cook. If you are a techie in the United States, it is likely too expensive to have a cook. Having said that, you can always learn to cook, at least simple dishes, because you control the quality of ingredients as well as the method of cooking by using less oil, or slow cooking.

- Drink more water. If you are not drinking enough water, you have absolutely no idea of what you are missing out on. Drinking water is even used as therapy. Though I haven't tried the therapy religiously, I have tried drinking a few glasses of water after I get up from bed. I don't gulp it down. I drink at a normal pace, until my body is comfortable. Initially, we might urinate, but the effect on the body is amazing. Just having water at proper intervals in the day has massive benefit.

What I suggested above is not some earth-shattering secret or expensive alternatives. These are simple things that can be done starting this moment.

Here's my final thought. Mind the stuff that goes into your body, because that's what shapes you. Always try to consume stuff that is natural or close to its natural state.

I believe health is more than saying mind your food. It's about the mind as well, and if your mindset is right, everything else will be right. And that's what we'll see next.

Food for your mind

Most of our problems related to health stem not just from eating habits, but also from our thoughts and behaviors. And that's why we need to be careful how we think and behave.

I have found that usually it is not the biggies that pull us down. It's common yet subtle things that pull us down. We all need to be very careful about the food we feed our mind. It can be dangerous to our health and wellness.

Be negative to negativity

Do you feel stressed out because of negative news?

Negativity sells, so the media uses it to make money. They really don't care about you. All they want is to hook you.

Each and every thing you see, read, and consume affects you in one way or another. It's how we develop our mental capacities. No wonder the world is becoming more chaotic than ever before even though the world seems to be at our fingertips.

I'm not saying that you should be ignorant or turn your face away when you see someone suffering. All I am saying is that mass marketing of negative news is designed to draw you in, and you end up not having the right mindset to pursue your things.

Negativity is like a bad smell, you don't know until you smell it, but you can always dilute it by using air fresheners such as reading useful books or working on projects with purpose.

Stop trusting everyone

I used to believe whatever was around me was true. Now I realize that whatever is being said or written is not entirely true.

Intentions and interests of politics, business, and economics drive it all.

Do you see constant news about a film actor in the newspaper or social media? Chances are that the actor's movie is slated for release in the coming weekend.

As they advertise, do you think drinking Coke or Pepsi will make you look cool? No, the sugar will make you fat, lazy, and more likely to have a heart attack. Ironically, drinking water will not make you look cool, but will cool your body.

Do you think by wearing that trendy outfit you'll look sexy? No, if you are out of shape, whatever you wear is not going to make you look like you are in shape. When you have a great body, even a simple and plain T-shirt will look great on you.

We discussed not being naive at work, but it's even more important not to be naive in life. That's why we need to always check the source of information and see if it makes sense.

If someone tells me that he is a life coach, and he is living alone in an old hut and a camper, I won't listen to his advice on life lessons.

If someone is advising me about becoming rich, and he is living in a rented house and driving used cars, I won't listen to his advice on becoming rich.

If someone is talking about dating and he has never taken a girl out for a date, I'll tell him to go on a date first and then advise others.

This someone can be anyone including friends, acquaintances, or gurus on the Internet. There are a lot out there. Just be careful and don't waste your time on such scammers. That's why you should always seek advice from people who have been there, done that, and have no obligation to say sugarcoated words to you.

Suppose you want to buy a house, go ask an independent real estate consultant who has a good track record and has invested in good properties. For advice on dating, go ask folks who do it all the time. For advice on career growth, go ask executives who are 10 years ahead of you in the path.

Some really high achievers such as CEOs, presidents, or Nobel Prize winners won't be accessible for advice. But you can still get their inputs and thoughts *by reading their books*. This strategy has been a game changer for me.

Find people who are ahead of you in life, and have done what you want to do. When you find them, just listen to them directly or indirectly, and *take massive action*.

Complaining is bad for health

You might feel frustrated that your peers got good offers; they are earning more money, taking vacations in Hawaii, or getting regular promotions.

You might feel if you had entered the industry 10 years earlier you would have done better. You might feel that everyone successful was present at the right place and at the right time.

Complaining is contagious. Once someone starts, everybody joins. The more we do, the more mileage we derive. I agree that there are a lot of issues in the industry. But so are there in other industries.

If someone is complaining about a techie job, they either don't know what doing other jobs feels like or have not gone through the slightest suffering in life. There are more challenging jobs that pay less. I am not saying that we should never complain.

Sometimes, it's okay to let out our emotions by complaining. All I am saying is that we should not let complaining get in our way. Have you heard people say the following?

- "I don't feel like working here. I don't have job satisfaction." *Do they even know what they want in life? Chances are, they don't. Then, how will they know what they want out of their job?*

- "I hate my job. They are paying to do stupid work." *By the way, who said jobs were created to give meaningful and enlightening work? Tell them to wake up. Jobs are created to do dirty work.*

- "This salary is a peanut. The CEO makes all the money." *Do they have the skillset to do the job of a CEO?*

- "My life sucks. I come early in the morning, work like a mule, and leave late at night." *Did they talk to their boss about this? Is this a problem of too much workload? Or is it a problem of taking long breaks and long lunches throughout the day?*

And the list goes on...

Once people start complaining, they won't stop complaining. It finds its way into all areas of your life. That's why it is so dangerous.

If you feel that you took a bad decision by joining company A, it's okay. What's the point of dwelling in the past and thinking, "If I had done that, life would have been much different"?

The very thing you control is NOW. What are you going to do about it?

One of the major effects of complaining is also one of the main killers of a techie's life. That's right, I am talking about stress.

How to handle stress

There are problems out there that are hurting you. Whether it is lack of job satisfaction, feeling stuck, not handling the work pressure, or relationship issues. Added to this, there could be long working hours and unrealistic expectations that can dampen your spirit.

And everything can lead to what we generalize as stress.

Stress usually occurs because of problems in our projects, problems with people, performance pressure, missed opportunities, fights with spouse, misunderstandings with close friends or family members, or any issues that hurt our value system.

Stress could manifest itself as sadness, frustration, lack of zeal in life, or any other trait that keeps you down. We stay late, eat junk, drink sodas, or booze around at night, and that leads to chain reactions, which cause havoc to our health.

Don't you think it is interesting the booze industry is always thriving irrespective of the economy? There's just so much stress in this world!

Apart from causing direct damage to our body, stress paves the way for us to develop toxic habits. We now know the power of habits. Imagine the havoc it can cause when habits are negative. And that's why it should be our highest priority to handle stress.

The following four tips really help as I have personally tested them.

1. Natural stress buster

Have you heard the golden goose story?

A farmer had a goose. One day, his goose laid a golden egg. He thought it was his luck. The next day, the goose laid another golden egg. Day after day, it laid a golden egg. He became greedy. His greed became so great that he cut the goose to get the all the eggs out of it. There were no golden eggs inside. The goose died and the farmer cried.

Can you identify who is the farmer, and who is the goose?

Well, we are both the farmer and the goose. Most of the time, we treat our body like the goose. We get greedy like the farmer and then wonder what the heck happened.

When I started working for Aetna at Hartford, Connecticut, I was handling five different applications—along with development, production support was under my plate. Daily jobs used to fail at night, and beepers kept buzzing at odd times. It was frustrating. In order to handle the pressure and stress, I made a major change to my life.

I stopped sleeping alone. I started to sleep with my laptop (sorry to disappoint, if you expected any other stress buster).

Sleep is the natural stress buster. And we cannot afford to miss it. Any machine if not maintained well will lose its production capacity after some time. Similarly, if we do not *sleep at least 8 hours a day*, our ability to perform degrades over time. We also have research supporting the importance of sleep. The following was reported in "Sleep inspires insight" published in the journal *Nature*:

> Subjects performed a cognitive task requiring the learning of stimulus–response sequences, in which they improved gradually by increasing response speed across task blocks. However, they could also improve abruptly after gaining insight into a hidden abstract rule underlying all sequences. Initial training establishing a task representation was followed by 8h of nocturnal sleep, nocturnal wakefulness, or daytime wakefulness. At subsequent retesting, more than twice as many subjects gained insight into the

hidden rule after sleep as after wakefulness, regard-
less of time of day. Sleep did not enhance insight in
the absence of initial training. A characteristic an-
tecedent of sleep-related insight was revealed in a
slowing of reaction times across sleep. We conclude
that sleep, by restructuring new memory representa-
tions, facilitates extraction of explicit knowledge and
insightful behavior.[1]

So it is evident that irrespective of sleep during daytime or night-
time, folks (who are trained) who had 8 hours of sleep perform better.

With the "innovation" of round the clock support, sometimes techies are even expected to work night shifts. I wouldn't fight the
system and screw my job. I'd try to wait for an opportunity to move
to a regular 9-5 schedule, or I'd just start looking for a different job
that does not mess up my sleep.

Sleep is such a natural stress buster. It's the must-have maintenance
for our body. I am not talking about getting up early in the morning,
doing yoga or exercises. Well, it will be awesome if do you that. But,
I am just asking you to make sure that you get 8 hours of sound sleep
every day. There is a magic that happens when you get a sound sleep
every day.

2. Channelize emotional energy

I remember the scene when I got an email that said my client work
permit did not go through. I locked my machine, walked downstairs,
and randomly walked trying to control the tears in my eyes. I went
to the side of the building so that nobody noticed.

Almost everyone got the client work permit in my peer group. Although no one was to blame, still I felt bad. All my friends were flying to work in the US one by one. I was caught up in confusion of

whether or not to dwell on the most-asked question, "Why me?"

There was a point when I would just stare at the monitor and only after an hour or so would I realize that I had not completed anything. I remember standing in front of a gas stove, heating milk and suddenly becoming teary-eyed. I remember getting jealous seeing my friends posting their photos on Facebook.

Others in my boat were quitting the company and going elsewhere for better pay. I did not have any motivation to join another company and yet was not motivated in my current work.

It was stressing me out.

Day by day my emotions were running high. I wanted to do something. It was reaching a point where my emotions were not controllable. It was hurting me. After seeing an advertisement on a weekend, I went to an NGO (Connecting in Pune, India) for suicide prevention. I went there to apply for a part-time volunteer position (for a second, didn't you think that I went there for other reasons?).

When I went there, I met amazing people from all walks of life who came forward to be of some help to society. I connected with a retired CEO, a retired teacher, a bookshop owner, a few physiotherapists, a stockbroker, and a few psychotherapy students. I was the only techie in that group of 30 who came forward to become a helpline volunteer.

However, there was a hurdle to become a volunteer. I had to undergo a 30-day training period and clear an interview. Well, I did undergo the training and did clear the interview. And they did reject people who were more experienced in life than me. I was a little embarrassed and yet proud that they selected me.

My job was to give two hours of phone support per week to people with suicidal thoughts and severe depression. It was tough. I was freaking out. After listening to their stories and giving them emotional support, I saw a different world around me.

After talking about suicide and death, clearly, my problem did not seem earth-shattering anymore. I was able to channelize my own emotional energy for a good cause and I was really glad I did that, because it benefited me more than anyone else. We'll see how in the next section.

3. **Reach out**

If there is one thing that we all strive for, it is to be perfect. We don't like to be laughed at, we don't like to be put in embarrassing situations, and we don't like to be seen as weak.

Kelly McGonigal, in her TED talk[2] "How to make stress your friend," says, "When life is difficult, your stress response wants you to be surrounded by people who care about you."

That is one way to handle stress: surrounding yourself with people who care about you. You might feel reaching out for help is a sign of weakness. It's not. Deciding not to reach out is a sign of weakness.

Most of the time, we need help. If you are not able to discuss issues with immediate family or friends, it is perfectly okay to reach out to a counselor or a psychotherapist. Many people don't do this, which leads to building up of stress levels and worsening of situations. Reaching out and talking to a counselor helps in most cases. It helps to heal the internal hurts and thoughts that could be leading to the stress. There is also another way and that's pretty cool. And you know what it is?

It is voluntarily reaching out and caring for others who are under stress.

I got so excited to know that our body is naturally designed to reduce our own stress levels when we reach out to others. Kelly went on to say in the same TED talk, "So when you reach out to others under stress, either to seek support or to help someone else, you release more of this hormone (*oxytocin*), your stress response becomes healthier, and you actually recover faster from stress. I find this amazing, that your stress response has a built-in mechanism for stress resilience, and that mechanism is human connection." This also proves why my work as a helpline volunteer helped me more than anyone else.

If reaching out is powerful, what's coming next is a much more powerful strategy to handle stress.

4. Pursue something exciting

After starting my career, for a few years I concentrated only on my office work. I would ignore all the activities in the world outside my work. To cite an instance, when I saw someone anchor on a stage, the child in me would say, "Rama, why are you not anchoring?" But the big boy in me said, "There are greater things to pursue in life. Better focus on that, buddy."

One day, I got an email at my office about a club called Toastmasters. It read that the club helps improve public speaking skills. I went there because public speaking was exciting to me. I was fascinated to see people giving awesome speeches. At that point, I realized that I never really boarded the train of my life.

I joined the community. I was surprised to see the amount of enthusiasm and inspiration I got while I worked on my speeches. My blood found new joy in circulation, alertness levels touched new heights, and each cell of my body displayed happiness.

I spent hours on my speeches—writing, rewriting, polishing, and practicing. Maybe it was the emotional build-up that I was channelizing. I also started competing in speech contests and even won one on my first try. When my manager heard this news, she bought it to the attention of my senior manager. After 15 minutes, I was called to my unit manager's room.

The big boss said, "We have our account's town hall event day after tomorrow and our IT heads of our client are visiting. I got a recommendation that you can host the event." After a pause, he said, "I have never seen you host, would you be able to host this crucial event?" Before my mind could analyze the situation, I said, "Yes, I will do it. Please let me know the details of the event." *I myself was surprised by the spontaneous reply.*

Everything seemed to have a connection. Out of nowhere, here I stood with an offer from my big boss to fulfill my childish desire. And maybe that was the reason the response came like a blitzkrieg.

Everything fell into place and there I stood behind the podium saying, "I welcome you all..." and greeting our client IT heads and unit heads. The event was a success and I received warm appreciations from my senior management.

I went on to win multiple contests, and I became one of the top six speakers in the entire India and Sri Lanka level, the first time I participated in a humorous speech contest.

In the meantime, my work permit got rejected a second time. But, I did not worry because I was having a lot of fun learning new skills. I became the president of the local chapter, tripling the club strength. I was having a lot of fun.

And the third time, my work permit and the US visa got approved.

And boy, I was much more confident. For me, public speaking is always exciting. That's probably why I kept competing in speech contests for many years and won more than 25 contests. Maybe, for you, tennis is exciting. For someone else, traveling to new places is exciting.

Find out what is exciting for you, and start doing it. If you feel music is exciting, listen to music. If you feel music is the thing, take it a step further by creating simple tunes.

If you are not sure, start off any activity for which you have an inclination. When I say inclination, you should feel an attraction, or should be naturally drawn to that activity.

Attracted to bird watching, or photography? Give it a shot. When you are watching a movie, or talking to a friend, or just simply sitting, if you ever get any thoughts like "I wish I could go to piano classes," just do it.

You never know where your excitement lies unless you try things out. Spending time on things that excite you is awesome. You won't feel the time passing by. Again, if you find your job exciting, then it is the best thing.

Sometimes, well, most of the time, it may NOT be exciting. So, it is your responsibility to find something that excites you.

And let me tell you that pursuing something exciting is the best way to beat stress, and naturally create powerful habits. And when you have tapped into the power of habits, you'll be mindful of *food for both your tummy and your thoughts*.

Thus leading, rather hacking your way to a healthy life.

And honestly, leading a healthy life is incomplete if you don't have a healthy relationship with your romantic partner, which is what we'll see next.

KEY TAKEAWAYS

- Habits create automation in human beings. It is crucial to develop keystone habits such as eating right or getting up in the morning for exercise.

192

- Prefer quality of food vs. quantity of food. Avoid prepackaged, processed, or fried food. Eat food in its natural state, and drink more water.

- Stay away from negativity; stop trusting everyone, and stop complaining.

- Always get inputs from people who have done what you want to do.

- Sleep for 7 to 8 hours per day.

- Channelize your emotional energy to create something. Reach out for help and reach out to help others.

- Pursue something exciting. This is like an antidote to fight mental, emotional, or physical health issues.

CHAPTER 10

ON ROMANTIC RELATIONSHIPS

In which, we'll see: how the society and system are flawed, controversial advice to attract a girl, what committed women want, how to manage attention struggles, why sex should be talked about, a reasonable theory that explains unreasonable fights, and tested strategies to reconcile after a fight

"We now ask our lovers for the emotional connection and sense of belonging that my grandmother could get from a whole village. Compounding this is the celebration of romantic love fostered by our popular culture. Movies as well as television soap operas and dramas saturate us with images of romantic love as the be-all and end-all of relationships, while newspapers, magazines, and TV news avidly report on the never-ending search for romance and love among actors and celebrities. So it should come as no surprise that people recently surveyed in the U.S. and Canada rate a satisfying love relationship as their number-one goal, ahead of financial success and satisfying career"—Dr. Sue Johnson, developer of Emotionally Focused Couple Therapy, and author of *Hold Me Tight*.

Before even I entered my school, the school authorities took a decision that would make me an illiterate. They decided to separate boys and girls and move them to different campuses. Nice.

Girls are awesome. They have the power to fire up a guy or water him down. There is no better motivation for a guy to perform at work or life than knowing that the girl he likes is watching him.

Guys are awesome. They are the reason why girls want to look beautiful. They are also one of the main reasons for a girl's motivation. Many girls work hard in part to prove that they are no less in competence.

And when these two species come together, it's just ecstatic. They experience feelings that they never knew existed within them. The feeling you get when you experience her breath, his caress, her possessiveness, his insecurity, her talkativeness, his silence, her love, his care... is just amazing.

It's such an important topic and yet the system in our society seems to be oblivious of it. I thought multiple times about whether I should be writing about this. Then, I thought someone should talk about it.

It is written from a guy's perspective. If you are a girl, you might find it helpful as well, but if nothing else, it should be a fun read, because I have resisted the urge to be politically right.

Illiterate by default

There seems to be a huge illiteracy when it comes to handling romantic relationships.

The education system is designed to teach a lot of things such as algebra, history, geography, mathematics, science, or any other not so useful subject for your adult life, but it misses an important subject—romance.

Why not romance as a mainstream subject like mathematics or science? Isn't romance one of the cornerstones of life?

I mean, everybody yearns to have a partner, everyone yearns to mate, and yet, despite the latest ultramodern technological advances happening in the world, this is not taught or even part of any mainstream system in the society.

Instead, we end up learning much about this important subject from a source we shouldn't learn from—movies. Movie production houses repeat love story after love story. If we learn romance from movies, we should be able to learn science by watching a sci-fi movie like *Interstellar*, right?

Another way we learn is by watching our parents. That might be a problem if our parents never got along with each other. What if they kept fighting with each other? What if they were divorced? So, rather than learning, the child gets scared to be in a relationship. Good.

What is the other option? Learn from friends. That might also be a problem because our friends are in the same boat.

Unless we are lucky enough to have the influence of a great couple, we are illiterates by default.

No wonder most teenagers and young adults end up exploring on their own and getting into all sorts of messes.

So, most of the time, we learn it the hard way, after getting into a relationship.

By no means am I a relationship expert or a dating guru or a couple's therapist. I am just a regular techie as vulnerable as you are.

However, I took a conscious decision to learn this stuff because it matters. I am writing what has worked for me and in general I found to be true from my observation.

Guys shouldn't chase girls

It has been portrayed in popular culture that a girl's main characteristic is her physical appearance. Even I used to believe it. Of course, the cosmetics industry wants women to buy more beauty products. But there seems to be mismatch between how males are designed and nature's natural design for females.

In many species, nature has designed males to be more attractive. It might sound controversial but let's take a step back and look at the animal kingdom. A lion is more attractive than a lioness. A peacock is more attractive than a peahen. Nature has built them that way.

I am not trying to be sexist here. A peahen or lioness is beautiful as well. But the design seems to be that the male of the species appears more attractive. Yet our world has conditioned guys to believe that girls are the ones who are attractive.

However, to be brutally honest, males have a natural urge to mate, and hence they chase after girls. Because of that urge, the ratio of guys chasing a girl is high. So, it becomes a matter of supply and demand. (And yet single girls might tell you that all the guys are taken or gay. So, it may also be a matter of perception.)

We know that when supply is less, demand becomes high. That's why girls hold the upper hand and guys give away the leverage. Actually, a guy can leverage a similar concept for his advantage. I'll come to it soon but before that, there is something important that every guy should know.

Every guy should first develop the mindset that he is the one who is made attractive by nature. It does not mean that a guy should develop ego and wait for a girl to come after him. But having this self-belief is going to increase his confidence like crazy.

Despite knowing all this, in order to be in a romantic relationship, a guy needs a girl. Rather than chase, the better approach is to attract her. So, let's start there.

How to attract her

I might get into trouble for saying this. Fame, money, looks are some common attraction factors. If you are a techie, chances are that you meet only one or none of the above factors. But here's the thing. Girls also get attracted to exclusivity and personality. So, I am going to share thoughts only on exclusivity and personality, because these aspects can be controlled unlike fame, money, or looks.

Exclusivity means being *different*. Personality can mean having a sense of humor and unpredictability, a highly desired attraction factor. So is confidence. The girl falls for the guy who seems to be in control. All the other things—looks, money, and fame—matter, but not as much as confidence. If you can get this right, you can get her.

Movies and romance novels have made it seem like an angel will come and change the guy's life. And I am a victim of this. I used to see a girl and go into la-la land, and start the romance even before saying a word to her. If I could start this process again, I would first find out whether she is even available for a relationship. I'd make this move fast and touch the reality because chances are that she is already committed or not interested in relationships at all.

We all know "All that glitters is not gold." All the girls (or even guys for that matter) who glitter are not gold either. You need to see if she sounds, thinks, and acts in the same way as you thought, and then decide to go after her (or him).

Don't worry, you won't run out of girls. At the end of the day, it's kind of a numbers game. We'll talk more about it in the last chapter.

So here's the strategy, which might sound controversial.

Once you decide that you want to go after the *one*, be around her but *don't make her feel* that you are going after her. Give the girls around her (maybe her friends or your friends in common) more attention. She should feel that you are giving attention to other girls around her. Make her comfortable and be respectful but don't make her feel important, especially when she is around other good-looking girls. In fact, you should show that you are having a good time with other women. This might sound controversial. Some women are wise to this and might dismiss the guy if the game isn't played well. But here's why this strategy so often works.

When other girls are having a good time with you, she'll know that you are charming and other women like you. This creates exclusivity.

What could be a better validation than other women liking you?

And then there is the concept of supply and demand. Since many girls have a good time being around you, your demand becomes high, and hence your value. Your *one* will notice, and you will hold the leverage.

Also, by not giving her any special attention and importance, you are making her feel insecure. There is no better pull than getting a feeling of something being taken away from reach. You are within her reach and might be taken away by other girls, and that's a powerful trigger.

She will be all messed up thinking, "Will I lose him?" If you can make her think this way, you are already halfway there. Even though there are 10 other guys chasing her, she will have a special thing for you, which we can very well call attraction.

If she makes a move, wait. Don't give in and for God's sake, don't end up saying "I love you" and asking to be in a relationship. She'll understand you planned it and she might, well, dump you.

Most girls are natural testers. They like testing you. Girls like such feelings of attraction, and they might keep testing you in various ways to make sure that these feelings are still active.

Most of them never tell you what they are actually thinking. They might act cute, or throw tantrums. Whatever it is, if you remain cool and composed, you won't fall for their games. And if you fail the test, the attraction will be lost.

Don't be surprised if you see or hear stories of nice guys (who buy flowers and chocolates) getting dumped by girls. Maybe she never had an attraction for nice guys. Maybe she felt he was only good for the "friend" or "service" zone. On the other hand, guys who are jerks can execute the above triggers and attract girls. That's why you should not be surprised to see or hear stories of girls hanging out with them.

While trying to be different, there are some basic qualities you shouldn't forget. Be courteous, and respectful. While walking with her: open the door for her, give her a hand when crossing the road, walk on the traffic-facing side of the curb.

But again the personality of cocky, cool, and confident will keep the attraction factor alive. Ask her out and before she can say no, say, "Just friends. Please don't have other thoughts." She'll be like, "What?"

Another way is that when you are asking her out, you have other options, but you shouldn't say that you have options. If she says NO when you ask her out, say "No problem" and keep it cool. Then take the other girl out. Then, the next time you meet her, talk about the time you had with the other girl. Don't make it obvious. Just say, "It was fun."

What do you think she is going to say when you call her up the next time? Either she'll call you names or she'll jump at the first opportunity to go out with you. Either way, it's good.

Use the above strategy with caution. It may not work on every girl and it can even backfire. I applied this technique to the girl I liked, who later became my GF. It impacted her so much that she started getting insecure whenever I talked with any girl. Not so good.

It took a long time for me to make her comfortable. By the way, I am married—same GF, not a different girl—now. I'll share more details on working a committed relationship in the next section.

You know your situation. You might find genuinely simple and straightforward girls as well. Trust your gut feeling. If you feel that she is just expecting you to make a move, give a little nudge. Again, don't push too much. It'll piss off any type of girl. I've done that (different girl... long ago... I'm clean now). Trust me.

What we have seen here are ideas to attract her into a relationship. This is just the trailer, the main movie starts when we commit to be in a relationship, and that's what we will see further.

What women want

"The great question that has never been answered, and which I have not yet been able to answer, despite my thirty years of research into the feminine soul, is 'What does a woman want?'" said Sigmund Freud, the renowned psychiatrist.

And yet, with the risk of making myself look like a fool, I am attempting to tackle this unsolvable mystery. Though I am not attempting to answer that overall question, I'll tackle a derivative of the question: What does a woman in a committed relationship want from her guy?

Whether in the West or East, there are certain traits that do not change, and here we go:

- She wants importance and expects you to have her as the first priority in your life.

- She wants attention and will go to any lengths to get it if you don't give it.

- She wants to talk and expects you to listen with undivided attention.

- She wants to share problems but does not want your solutions.

- She wants surprises and gifts though not necessarily expensive ones.

- She wants appreciation.

- She wants to be pampered a lot.

- She wants you to make her feel awesome in bed.

- She wants you to support her when someone calls out her mistake.

- She wants you to say sorry even though it was her fault.

- She wants you to be by her side so that she will feel secure.

- She wants you to love her like crazy.

- She wants you to respect her for who she is and what she likes.

- She wants you to protect her dignity against any odds.

Man, this is so much to ask. I sometimes feel this is more pressure than I feel from work or any of my projects.

Let me share a story of a husband and a wife. I'll leave it up to you to assume whether this happened with me. Husband is driving, and wife is sitting in the passenger seat, and they are going home after work on a Friday evening.

Husband is humming "You and I in this beautiful world. Green grass, blue skies."

Wife: "I don't know. Folks are not being productive. They do not understand anything that I am saying. I am getting exhausted."

Husband: "It's Friday. Just chill."

Wife: "You are not understanding what I am saying." Husband is thinking: *What is there to understand here?*

Husband: "Okay. I thought you were getting stressed."

Wife: "Yes, I am stressed but these people at work don't understand anything that I am saying."

Husband stops humming. He is thinking why is she saying the same thing again and again. And why is she not leaving the matter.

The fact is guys are solution oriented, and girls are feelings oriented. I realized this the hard way. I confirmed this when I read John Gray's bestselling book *Men Are from Mars, Women Are from Venus.*

The truth is she does not want solutions. She just wants you to listen.

"Listening" is the solution. If you show genuine interest in what she is saying with an occasional acknowledgment, she will be excited. I know. I know. This is really hard for guys. But, if you have married a girl, it is part of the package!

Don't get caught up with the BS mindset that you don't feel like listening. If you don't feel like it, fake it. At work, do you feel like doing all the crap that comes along?

It's the same for your relationship. See this as an effort to improve your romantic life. It takes effort. Heck, anything worthwhile takes tons of effort.

Without knowing the above facts, the husband might innocently say, "I told you to chill to come out of the stress. Why are you are saying the same problem again?"

And the wife goes, "Why are you getting irritated?"

And the husband feels his blood pressure rising. Sadly, he doesn't even know that his wife has already shifted the problem from "stress at office" to "My husband does not have time for me." This is not the case with just career-oriented women. She could be a student, or a homemaker, but that does not mean she will expect *less*.

The "stress at office" problem will manifest into problems because of school, in-laws, boredom, or any topic in the universe.

The attention struggle

One of my close friends is a techie at a blue-chip company. More than that, he developed a passion for photography. He started doing fashion photography. Meanwhile, he liked a girl.

They started seeing each other and got committed in a romantic relationship. After a few years, he became a wildlife photographer! The story did not here.

He got engaged to her but the marriage was postponed because of an emergency in her family. Then that marriage never happened because of the growing divide in their relationship.

Years later he told me: "I think that relationship broke because she felt that I was giving more importance to photography."

Now, after a few years of marriage, I agree that girls want to feel important. A guy or a girl in a relationship will be possessive and seek attention. That's perfectly okay.

But we should also realize that we need to give space to each other or the relationship can become suffocating.

It makes me smile when I think that my wife still thinks that there are girls out there who are trying to pick me up. Though, that's not true! And another fun fact, her main enemy is my MacBook Pro. She feels I spend more time with my MacBook than with her.

To mitigate such false feelings, you should give her attention and make her feel important.

After marriage, the attention struggle might become severe. The power struggle could be between your spouse and immediate family such as mom, dad, siblings, or very close friends. Again there are no hard and fast rules on who is at fault.

Everyone could be really nice. It is their role that creates the power struggle. It seems to be the law of nature. Most of my time goes to managing the attention that my wife and dad seek from me.

My college buddy said something that I found really amusing. He said, "When I entered college, you guys reduced my anger meter. When I became a husband, the anger meter reduced to really low levels. After my son was born, my anger meter has hit rock bottom."

The only person who has to be smart is *you* because you are the variable. Though I haven't found any step-by-step guide—I'll be the first to buy if there is one—to handle this power struggle, you will be good if you:

- Make your spouse feel as if she or he is your first and most important priority.

- Talk to your immediate family about it, and ask them to help you. But give them a feeling that you are there for them, which is what your immediate family members want.

If you can make sure that you are aligning to the above rules without hurting your immediate family or close friends, you'll be fine.

Now, it's time to talk about a topic that rarely gets the attention it deserves.

Let's talk about sex

Ok, so here is the taboo topic. Sex seems to be the biggest irony. Everybody wants it or is involved with it, but very few openly talk about it. The culture is more open in the West than the East. Especially, in India where everybody—parents, teacher, neighbor, cab driver, CEO, or techie—will talk about cricket (it could easily qualify as the biggest religion in India) though a small percentage of the people actually play it. Meanwhile nobody talks about sex, but people seem to love it. India did not become the democracy with the largest population so easily. A lot of people did a lot of work.

And if the topic comes up at all, we close the doors, lower our voice, become shy, or move our heads left and right to check if anyone is listening. Why is it such a taboo topic?

It is not supposed to be a taboo topic. Or else, why would Napoleon Hill identify sex as the tenth step towards riches and as the #1 stimuli of the mind—ahead of love, fame, power, and money—in *Think and Grow Rich,* which is one of those rare books that have passed the test of time to emerge as a perennial bestseller. He wrote, "Sex desire is the most powerful of human desire. When driven by this desire, men develop keenness of imagination, courage, will power, persistence, and creative ability unknown to them at other times. So strong and impelling is the desire for sexual contact that men freely run the risk of life and reputation to indulge it. When harnessed, and redirected along other lines, this motivating force maintains all of its attributes of keenness of imagination, courage, etc., which may be used as powerful creative forces in literature, art, or in any other profession or calling, including, of course, the accumulation of riches."

If you have problems in your romantic relationship, chances are that the root cause is lack of proper sex. Honestly, ask yourself if your physical needs are met? If not, it is high time to take action. You might not even know how it is affecting you.

Talk to your partner openly about your needs. Avoid thoughts of "He should understand me" or "She should know my needs." There is no point in holding up because of ego, shame, or shyness. It's okay to let down your ego and talk about your needs. After all, your spouse or romantic partner has decided to be with you for the rest of your lives! That's a really big move.

A good sexual relationship is like a master solution to a lot of relationship problems. It'll even boost your performance in other areas.

I also believe this is a skill, which takes proper know-how and practice like any other skill. I cringe about this. How are we supposed to learn it as a skill?

There are paths of having one-night stands or paying money. I neither had the guts to take this not-so-desirable-sometimes-illegal path nor did the work to be in a live-in relationship. And my GF considered premarital sex as a sin. So, it made me a pure virgin until I got married (*I know. It's horrible*). It's like running your code for the first time directly in production without any testing.

I think we should be adults and inhibit the sense of awkwardness. If needed, it might also be a good idea to take professional help. We should do whatever it takes to get this going, because it is essential and it matters.

If sex is something that needs to be handled, so is fighting. There are couples that never fight. But it is unavoidable for most couples. And that's what we'll see next.

How to handle fights

Before learning how to handle fights, let us understand why unreasonable fights happen, using a simple example.

Husband says, "I am not finding my shirt."

Wife goes, "Why do you always blame me if you can't find your shirt?"

Husband is thinking: *What the heck is she talking about?* And says, "When did I blame you? And why are you behaving like a child?"

She goes, "Why are you getting irritated?" That's enough for the husband to get really irritated.

And let the unreasonable fight begin...

Have you faced such situations? More importantly, have you tried to understand why this happened in the first place?

There is a theory that can explain this. It really helped me and I believe it will really help any couple. Transactional analysis (TA) is a psychoanalytic theory and a method of therapy wherein social transactions are analyzed to determine the ego state of the patient (whether parent-like, child-like, or adult-like) as a basis for understanding behavior. Eric Berne coined it.[1]

To help you understand, I'm super simplifying this theory. We have the following ego states as we grow up. Parent ego state (taught concepts), Adult ego state (learned concepts), and Child ego state (felt concepts).

And, we get into one of these states even now. Let us analyze the example. The husband said, "I am not finding my shirt" from a typical Adult ego state, thinking that it would reach his wife's Adult ego state.

He expected her to help him find his shirt. But unfortunately, her Child ego state was activated. Maybe, as a child, her parents blamed her for not keeping her clothes properly folded, and hence the Child ego state got activated and she said, "Why do you always blame..."

When the husband hears his wife talk about blaming, his Parent ego gets activated and he tries to correct her by saying, "Why are you behaving like a child?"... *And the fight starts.*

It became a fight because the husband's Parent ego state is talking to his wife's Child ego state, which is a cross transaction.

According to transactional analysis theory, interactions are smooth during complementary transactions and not smooth (a fight) during cross transactions. Hence the fight started between the husband and wife.

Now, that I have at least shed some light on things that might have always puzzled you, let's try to find ways to leverage this concept.

We now know that fights or conflicts can be avoided when we *complement the transactions.*

This means that the transactions (the conversations) should be between Adult ego and Adult ego, Child ego and Child ego, or Parent ego and Parent ego for the communication to be smooth.

The conflict comes when cross transactions happen, as shown in the example above. The Parent ego state of the husband talking to the Child ego state of his wife is an invitation to destroy the day!

At least from my experience, new wives or girlfriends are like kids seeking your attention all the time. Not that new boyfriends or husbands don't seek attention!

Either way, be equipped to complement transactions by getting into Child ego state when needed. You can try to be in Adult ego state, but Child is more effective as you can make her laugh or smile. What you should absolutely avoid is being in Parent ego—advise or correct—state. It's a recipe for a fight.

Till now, we saw fights from a theoretical point of view. Now, let's see them from a practical point of view. You are having a fierce fight. You feel she is going over the top, bringing in all sorts of points that do not make any sense.

Some favorites of mine from experience: "God is there for me," "I am not a dog to keep coming at the back of you," "Don't think that you are the best person in this whole world."

But, that's the moment you need to observe. When she starts making illogical points that means she is asking you: "Are you there for me?" "Can I trust you?" "I am falling; can you hold me?" That's the moment you need to step down your ego—though it is really hard to do—and pause for a few seconds. And then, HUG HER. This is very powerful and has worked wonders for me. She might push you, but hold her tight. This is a great way to answer her unspoken questions.

Again, even guys get illogical and insecure. And when his woman hugs him, it's more powerful than any amount of words to bring him back.

Dr. Sue Johnson wrote in *Hold Me Tight*, "This drive to emotionally attach—to find someone to whom we can turn and say 'Hold me tight'—is wired into our genes and our bodies. It is as basic to life, health, and happiness as the drives for food, shelter, or sex."

Sometimes, rather most of the time, neither you nor your spouse or partner will make the first move to solve the fight. Are you holding on to your stance that your spouse is wrong?

Do you think you'll win by proving it as well? No way.

You'll actually wield more power when you allow yourself to lose, and make the first move. It took me a lot of time to understand this. There is a magic that'll happen when you are ready to let down your ego stance, and comfort your spouse. Your spouse will also realize and change slowly.

Apart from this, regular love, patience, honesty, and openness will immensely help your relationship. Working a romantic relationship takes effort, but I believe if you apply the above concepts, you'll be in a much better position than current levels.

Now that we dealt with "honey," it's time to deal with "money." As cliché as it sounds—it's all about the money, honey.

KEY TAKEAWAYS

- There is no proper system to teach the subject of romantic relationships. It rests upon us to educate ourselves because romance is as important to life as our career.

- Nature has designed males of many species to be more attractive. Guys should not chase girls. Instead, guys should attract girls using confidence, personality, and psychology.

- A woman wants attention and importance from her man. She does not want his solutions. She wants him to listen, appreciate, love, and care for her.

- During an attention struggle, give priority to your romantic partner. Seek help from your immediate family to support your relationship, but let them know that you are there for them.

- Sex with your romantic partner is important. Lack of it could lead to other problems. Proper sex can strengthen your relationship and even increase your performance in life.

- According to transactional analysis, cross transactions lead to misunderstandings while complementary transactions lead to smooth communication. You'll win her by losing the fight.

CHAPTER 11

MONEY IS NOT THE PROBLEM

In which, we'll see: why "study well, get a good job" is flawed advice, four counterintuitive ideas for being frugal, how to manage debt and taxes, how to create assets without investing a lot of money, and how techies can create passive income

Oscar Wilde once said, "When I was young I thought that money was the most important thing in life; now that I am old I know that it is." While I was growing up, my dad did not give me necessary things like money but he gave me a lot of unnecessary things like advice. He used to say, "Study well, get a good job, you can buy anything you want."

I studied well and got a good job. But, the things I wanted always cost more money. Don't you think that the things you really, really want always cost a little more money? Think about it—that beautiful house, that beautiful car, that beautiful vacation (full marks if you thought I would say "beautiful girl") always cost a little more money.

Money is not the problem. Lack of more money is always the problem.

We techies live in a bubble of richness. For some reason, society believes that all software techies are rich. There are techies who get really fat paychecks. These techies are either responsible for critical enterprise level software or they are directly responsible for increasing the employer's profits. They are the exception, not the norm. Let's talk about the norm.

Do we have financial freedom? As in, if we stop working tomorrow, will our life still be the same?

We earn enough money to visit high-end restaurants, buy Levi's jeans and Nike shoes, go for a vacation to the Himalayas or Hawaii, and drink vodka during the weekends. We can also get a car from Hyundai or Honda. But, how will you buy your dream house? We have a solution—a mortgage!

We techies seem to be the cash cow for multiple industries and the government. They don't just milk money in taxes taken out of our paychecks, but feed us junk food, get us to buy unnecessary stuff in super-sized malls, lock us in heavy mortgages, lure us into expensive vacations, hit us with heavy hospital bills, and still collect taxes on all these expenses. Nice.

Finally, we look like a superhero with a huge credit card bill. And end up being poor.

In India, a decent, spacious 3-bedroom apartment will cost around 1 crore rupees in any good city, even in suburban areas. And if you want a premium apartment in a premium location, you need a minimum of 2 to 4 crore Indian rupees, which is roughly about 300,000 to 600,000 USD.

Now, if you are in the US, this is plenty of money in most areas to buy a nice house with a yard big enough to have a barbecue party. For a techie working in the US, a nice sedan costs 3 to 4 times the monthly salary, and a house is 3 to 4 times the yearly salary.

However, it's not the same factor for a techie working in India. The factor is 10 to 12 times. A nice sedan is 10 to 12 times the currently monthly salary, and a good house (not a dream house) is again 10 to 12 times the yearly salary.

And I did not even talk about INFLATION in India. The price of groceries, vegetables, clothes, and every other damn thing is increasing in double digits per year except one thing—salary. Inflation is so high that the career growth story of a techie working with a big software tech company in India has become a joke. So, it is apparent that what my dad said, "Study well, and get a good job," is flawed.

And that's why we need to be a little smart about money, which we will see in the coming sections.

Embrace frugality

How many clothes do you have in your closet that you do not wear?

How many appliances are in your house that you hardly use?

How many pairs of footwear are untouched in your shoe rack?

Do you like to buy stuff but hardly use it? I confess that I was not Buddha either.

In 2012, I went to a Hyundai car showroom in New Jersey to buy my first car. I was checking out all the cars and the salesman was saying the usual BS. I chose a grey Hyundai Elantra with a cool sports mode (and paid more money). Something you should know which I am not proud of: I never used that sports mode even once.

I'm not a big fan of living in strict financial limits by saving on coffees and pennies. But, lately I have realized that I should not buy or even get free stuff that I don't need.

Buy what you need

The other day, I met my school friend after a long while. The last time I met him, he had a new phone. And now, he had another phone. And you know the size of the phone? It was around 8 inches. I am not kidding. It was just few inches short of a tablet.

I asked him, "Why did you buy this?" He goes, "I got a good offer to exchange my old phone." And I asked, "How does it fit into your pocket?" He goes, "That seems difficult. Even I am figuring it out."

These days, technology and systems encourage impulse buys. Things that we buy based on wants rather than needs. The world wants you to spend more money on your wants.

But, you'll be smart if you spend money on your needs.

I think the only reason you should buy is based on what is essential. And only you'll know what is essential for you.

If you already have five pairs of shoes, do you really need one more? If you have 20 outfits, do you need more clothes? If you are getting stuff that you really don't need for a 90 percent sale, is it worth it?

When Microsoft Surface was launched, I was one of the first buyers of the tablet. At that time, I had an HP Envy laptop, I had an HTC EVO 4G phone but since owning a tablet seemed to be a cool thing, I bought one. Then, this happened.

If I wanted to browse or work on anything, my laptop was comfortable. If I had to check something quickly online, my phone was comfortable. After a month or so, I realized I could not fit that gadget to my lifestyle. I really did not know why I bought that tablet.

So, one fine day, when the essentialist in me woke up, I sold it on eBay. The guy who bought it left a comment that I am proud to share, "I wanted to gift this to my girlfriend. It looks so new. Seems like you never used it. Thank you so much."

And I am glad that I let go, which is usually not easy. We'll see why and how.

Let stuff go

Greg McKeown shared a research finding in *Essentialism*. Researchers gathered 100 students. Fifty students were given a coffee mug and told that you own this coffee mug. The researchers asked the students to quote a price if they wanted to sell it. The next 50 students were shown the same coffee mug and asked to quote a price to buy the same.

The first 50 students did not quote below $5.25, whereas the other 50 students did not quote above $2.25. The experiment was conducted to understand the psychology of ownership.

Do you see the psychology of people when they OWN something?

The value becomes higher if you own it.

And that's why we do not let go of the things that we own. However, you'll be doing yourself a favor when you let go of stuff that you don't need.

If you are not able to decide to let go of something because you bought it for a lot of money, ask the question, "If I was going to buy this today, how much would I be willing to pay?"

If the answer is "nothing," give it away.

Declutter the things that you haven't used for more than six months to a year. If you haven't worn an outfit for so long, chances are that you will not in future either.

Say NO to things that do not add any value to your real life, whether it is a material thing, or a social invitation, or peer pressure, or randomly seeing Facebook posts.

Now that we have talked about letting go of stuff, I want to talk about a counterintuitive concept that you might have experienced but not realized.

Cheap is also expensive

Cheap is not cheap. Most of the time, it turns out to be expensive. I'll illustrate this soon but be careful of people selling cheap products or services.

If you buy a used car, you spend money on maintenance, low performance, and fuel consumption. The impacts can cascade. You can suffer breakdowns on the road, which will cost you in office time, and might cause you to miss an important meeting.

Clearly, the known and unknown costs seem to be expensive. But if you pay a premium price and buy a good car, you'll spend less money on fuel, less time and money on maintenance, and have reliable transportation and more peace of mind.

A cheap price does not mean it is not expensive, and a premium price does not mean it is expensive.

You can take your girlfriend on a date to a mediocre place, just because it's cheap. If she figures that out, it might cost you that budding relationship, which is expensive.

You can buy a laptop with Mac OS, at a premium compared to a Windows laptop. With the high possibility of a crash or a virus attack on the Windows laptop and the associated waste of time, the Mac laptop does not seem to be expensive. I am not a Windows hater or a Mac lover, but I hope you get the point.

It all boils down to this: we can pay the premium price for things we absolutely need, or absolutely love. But, we can ruthlessly cut down on things that we don't need, even if they are cheap or free.

Save more

I used to spend like a maniac when I started working in the US. I kind of knew that I was getting out of control but did not have the self-reliance to stand up and change things around.

That's when I realized the need to be mindful of my money. If I started again, I'd save at least 10 percent of my income. Probably, a little more since I wouldn't be having family commitments.

There is no limit. Just do the damn savings. It will be very useful when needed. And one good strategy is to automate it because we won't do it manually month after month (come on, you know this).

Automate the savings by arranging a direct debit on a specific date from your main salary account to a separate savings account (common in the US) or into a recurring deposit (which is common in India).

If we don't save in a separate forced account, the money suckers will take it away.

Managing money suckers

I am not an MBA in finance from Harvard or Indian School of Business (ISB). And I believe you don't need to be one to manage your money. If nothing else, I really want you to manage these money suckers.

Clear debt

When reporters asked Warren Buffett, one of the most successful investors in the world, what's your advice for young people, he said, "Stay away from credit cards." I love what he said because credit cards create debt. The entire mortgage and credit card industry thrives on this sucker. The trap is so simple, and yet we fall for it.

Why should we borrow money to buy things that are not absolutely needed? And yet, especially in the US, credit history is given very high importance in many financial transactions. What it means is that you should have taken credit, and paid it back properly, whether it was a mortgage or a credit card bill.

The system is forcing you to use credit.

And that's okay, as long as you are paying off all the credit card expenses before the due date. But if you are surviving off credit card debt, it's an alarm.

First things first, pay off your credit card. That's the worst sucker. Really, it just sucks you out of energy. If you have a mortgage, do whatever it takes—start a side gig or work part-time at a second job—to clear it off or reduce the monthly payments. At least bring it to a level where you don't feel the pressure of carrying your house on your shoulders.

It is absolutely crucial that you follow the above as a cardinal rule. Unless you do it, you are not even at square one. In the next section, I'll talk about assets and passive income, which are game changers when it comes to earning money.

But before that, let's learn about the other money sucker—taxes.

Reduce taxes

I never thought about taxes when I started working. I was happy that somebody was paying me money, and money was getting deposited in the bank.

Only recently, I was reflecting on the concept and I found it really interesting. Out of every 100 bucks that we earn, we are directly paying a percentage to the government, which is kind of fair because they also need money to run the nation.

In most places, we pay taxes on all the other things that we buy as well. Essentially, we are paying double tax to the government!

So, it is our responsibility to at least reduce the direct tax that gets cut as part of our paycheck.

This topic might be boring, but ignorance of how taxes work might hurt you bad. Whether you are in India or the US, your employer will start deducting the tax amount and depositing the same in a government-authorized bank on a regular basis (maybe monthly or quarterly).

The year-end filing is just a way to reconcile the final math. If your employer paid more tax than needed during the course of the year, you can claim a refund after the year-end filing. If your employer underpaid taxes for you during the year, you owe a check to the government tax authorities.

India tax system: If you are working in India, I want you to understand how taxes work. The tax is calculated based on income brackets. For easy illustration, I am going to make up the numbers: no tax until 25 bucks. Ten percent tax for income between 25 and 50 bucks, 20 percent tax for income between 50 and 100 bucks, 30 percent tax for income above 100 bucks.

Based on above brackets, if your taxable income is 110 bucks, can you calculate the tax that you'll pay? It'll be the addition of 0, 2.5, 10, and 3 bucks, which equals 15.5 bucks.

I just made up these numbers to help you understand how tax brackets work. The actual tax brackets and the percentages might vary based on income and other factors for the year. Please refer to current documentation in the government website or any authentic sources.

During the year-end, the employer issues Form-16 and Salary Certificate that helps us understand how much salary was drawn during the year, and how much taxes are already paid to the government.

US tax system: If you are in the US, it gets more complicated. It would be overkill if I try to simplify the personal tax system in the US, but here's the gist. There will be a direct debit of taxes from your paycheck to the federal government, state government, and possibly the city as well. Exactly how much is withheld will vary based on your salary, your marital status, where you live, and even the state where you work, and lot more factors. You need to fill out and give a W4 to your employer so that the employer starts taking out taxes.[1]

During the year-end, the employer issues a W2 form that helps us understand how much salary was drawn during the year, and how much taxes are already paid to the government.[2] The brackets and numbers change based on your state, local, and national tax laws and your current salary.

Now, let's talk about reducing taxes. There are many options. When we say options that'll reduce taxes, what it means is: *when you invest in any of these options, that money will not be considered taxable income*. For example, in India, one option is to invest in a tax-saving equity plan. If you invest 10 bucks from your income of 110 bucks, then your taxable income will reduce to 100 bucks. In the US, the additional money you put in 401(K) and health savings accounts, for example, will not be taxable.

There are so many options and I honestly don't want to give the options because it varies based on your salary, situation, and status. I'd recommend that you talk to a tax professional or financial planner. Most tax professionals are called CPA (certified public accountant) in the US, CA (chartered accountant) in India. It just makes sense to talk to professionals and use their services. Let them understand your salary structure and company benefits, and advise you on reducing your tax liabilities and making investments that meet your long-term goals.

While hiring a professional, please check whether the consultant has a good track record for *reducing tax liability*. I would suggest finding someone who does tax consultation and can suggest *sound tax-saving investment options that meet your long-term goals.*

If you want to improve your financial literacy, which I highly recommend, check out Ramit Sethi's *I Will Teach You to Be Rich*. This will be helpful for people working and getting a salary in the US. This is a practical and fun book to read. Only after reading this book did I realize that I can call a bank representative and ask them to reverse any fee debit. I never thought it was an option. Bank of America applied a $10 fee for overdraft. I called them up and asked for a reversal, and boom, the fee debit got credited back. Since then, I never miss an opportunity to call the bank or my credit card provider to reverse any late payment fee.

If you are getting a salary in India, then I'd like you to check out *13 Steps to Bloody Good Wealth* by Sunil Dalal and Ashwin Sanghi. It is a very good book for beginners to get the basics right.

Again, I would highly recommend that you seek the advice of an expert with a good track record to reduce taxes and suggest investment options. But, I also recommend that you be equipped with the bare minimum knowledge.

If you are in the US, put as much money as possible in a 401(K) account. If you are in India, you can put the maximum amount in NPS (National Pension Scheme) and VPF (Voluntary Provident Fund). Some companies match this amount, and that's pretty cool. If they do not, never mind, because this money will be deducted at the source before the salary becomes taxable.

Interest on mortgage payments is not taxable. House rent, up to a certain limit, is not taxable (only in India). Education loans, travel allowances (depends on company), moving expenses, and certain work-related costs may not be taxable.

Apart from the above, you can always invest in tax-saving equities or bonds based on your risk appetite.

Till now, we only saw how to manage and optimize salary income. But, if we want to really reach financial freedom, it's time that we learn about assets.

Invest in assets

Let us talk about assets and liabilities.

Don't let the simplicity fool you: an asset increases your net worth whereas a liability decreases your net worth. It took a lot of time for me to understand them. They are powerful.

Assets help you generate money and in addition, their monetary value may increase over time. Liabilities will suck money out of you and in addition, their monetary value may decrease over time. If you want to know whether something is an asset, use the above definitions to find the answer.

Here's the cool part. Assets and liabilities are concepts. We ideally should not attach these labels to an entity. For example, owning an apartment with a mortgage, but collecting a monthly rental, is an asset. However, owning an apartment with a mortgage, with no income, is a liability.

Robert Kiyosaki, in his bestselling book *Rich Dad Poor Dad,* brilliantly wrote, "The philosophy of the rich and poor is this: the rich invest their money and spend what is left. The poor spend their money and invest what is left. Rich people acquire assets. The poor and middle-class acquire liabilities that they think are assets. An asset puts money in your pocket. A liability takes money from your pocket."

If you have understood the above concepts, where will you invest money? I can hear you say, "Of course, assets."

Many people fret that they do not have money to invest in real estate. Real estate is not the only asset in the world. A software, app, book, or website can all qualify as assets provided they make money.

You don't need a lot of money to build these assets. You can start small and scale up slowly. In today's world, you can start off with very little budget.

But you need to use the not-so-secret resources: intelligence, effort, and time. As a techie, you have already proved yourself. And I bet that you are not short of intelligence or effort. Time is always figure-out-able.

Many people get caught up in investor funding, angel funding, and a zillion other reasons not to take action on their ideas. I did not say it, but I second Mark Cuban, one of the self-made billionaires in the world, when he shared that opinion during an interview.[3] He said, "Just. Just go after it. I mean the thing about being an entrepreneur is it's just all to you. You know, a lot of people like to make excuses. 'I don't have connections. I don't have money. I don't have this.' But you know, if you find something that you like to do or love to do, be great at it and you'll be good. In worst case, you are going to have fun doing what you love to do and best case you can turn it into a business. I am just not big on excuses."

When the host asked for his thoughts about taking a loan, Mark said, "First of all, if you are just starting a business and taking a loan, you are a moron. There are so many uncertainties involved in starting a business and yet the one certainty you have is to pay back your loan. And the bank does not care about paying back your loan or whoever you borrowed from, unless it is family. It is just complete conflict."

And when the host persisted to know how to handle the capital part, Mark said, "99 percent of the small businesses don't fail for the lack of capital. They fail because of lack of brains, or they fail because of lack of effort. Most people don't put in the time to work smart. If you start a business, you better know your industry and company better than anyone else in the world because you are competing. And to think that whoever that is you are competing with is going to let you come in and take their business, obviously that's just naive."

If you are already an expert at something, start from there. Let us say that you are good at coding. Think how you can use that expertise to build an app and add value to someone.

Mark Zuckerberg used his coding skills to build something fun called Facebook. Now Facebook serves more than 1 billion or probably 2 billion people around the world.

What I am trying to say is you don't need to borrow money to build assets. You can build assets by bootstrapping your idea with your own money, time, and effort.

A few things you can do: invest in solid stocks, and/or create books, apps, or digital or physical products that sell. Physical products have a bit of hassle but if you have an idea that involves physical products, you should test your idea.

Do you know why I am stressing assets so much? It's because they have the power to create passive income.

Creating passive income

You might have heard about *passive income*. Hearing this concept is not enough. It is worth eating, chewing, and completely digesting. Passive income is where the money you earn is not directly proportional to the time you spend. Only a few percent of people achieve this. This contrasts to the traditional way of earning money.

The traditional way of earning money is through active income. Techies working as employees get active income. We log stipulated hours per month and get paid. The money is directly proportional to the time spent at the workplace.

Investors, business owners, and even authors earn passive income. I am not using the word entrepreneur because entrepreneurs can fall into active income or passive income.

A freelance yoga teacher who does personal yoga training is an entrepreneur. He gets active income because the more clients he teaches, the more money he makes.

However, another yoga teacher who has five yoga studios is also an entrepreneur, but she earns passive income. In this case, the income she earns is not dependent on whether she teaches yoga. She has built a system where yoga teachers and students come together and practice at her studios.

Yes, she will have some work to do but the income generated is not linearly proportional to her time, and that's why it is passive income. I don't know anyone other than network marketing folks who exploit the passive income concept like crazy.

They say it is easy to create millions by just working few hours a week, and they bash your job. And yet the truth is you need to work your butt off to succeed in network marketing. If you have tried network marketing, you might have realized that your techie job is a cakewalk.

There are people who are successful in network marketing. But, they portray that network marketing is the only game in town to earn passive income, which is a true lie.

The rules have changed. The world is getting flatter and flatter. You don't need connections. You don't need permission of gatekeepers.

You can use the power of the Internet and technology to build real value out there and earn passive income.

You can create passive income through affiliate marketing, monetizing a blog, monetizing a YouTube channel, self-publishing books, selling courses, running membership sites, selling apps, and a lot of other ways. There are many more options but for the ones above, you don't need a lot of money to get started.

Of course, you need to spend some money for buying courses, coaching, and infrastructure setup. But, this money is like peanuts compared to the money you'll spend enrolling in a traditional B-school or starting a traditional business.

There is overwhelming information out there. That's the main problem. But trust me, it is not rocket science. If someone like me can publish six books including this, you can very well do something similar.

But don't think I got up one day from sleep and decided, "Rama, you are going to write books and become a successful author."

NO.

Heck NO.

I first tried my hand at network marketing. I did everything, well, maybe not everything. Just being honest. I failed but learned a lot of invaluable and painful lessons.

My ego wouldn't let me sleep. I wanted to find other ways of creating passive income and thus began my journey. I searched for "making money online" in Google.

I found the Chris Farrell membership site that promised to teach me how to make money online. They taught affiliate marketing through ClickBank.

Affiliate marketing is where you promote other people's digital products for a commission. You can promote using email, blog, or social media.

Though I learned many concepts, I did not feel like promoting products in ClickBank. But I learned about website creation, list building, using email auto responders, and a lot more.

Then, someone said YouTube is the in-thing. I bought a course on YouTube marketing from Gideon Shalwick. I asked my friend to shoot my videos... giving public speaking tips, not anything else.

YouTube can be leveraged in many ways. But if you want to monetize it, your videos need to serve a set of people. Based on the location of the audience, number of views, and a few other factors, YouTube will pay you.

I posted the videos on YouTube and this continued for a few months. Then, someone told me blogging is the in-thing.

I felt that I need a professional blog setup. So, I bought a premium WordPress theme called OptimizePress. I started writing blogs.

Blogging allows you to show your expertise. And Google will index your articles if they are good. When people search for related key words, your blog posts will show up organically in search results.

Blogging went on for a few months, but then I saw people creating courses on platforms such as Udemy. I got excited.

Course creation is where you teach skills or give valuable information for which people are ready to pay. It can be a set of videos, audios, checklists, or worksheets.

I created few courses in Udemy. Udemy is a marketplace, which means your course will be competing with hundreds of similar products. I tried to work on making it big in Udemy, but then someone told me about Product Launch Formula by Jeff Walker.

Instead of enrolling into the PLF program, I bought *Launch*, his bestselling book.

The basic assumption of PLF is that you need to have a list of email subscribers. PLF is a serialized way of selling where you send 3 to 5 touch points (through emails or blog posts or videos) to your subscribers and add value to them. During the second or third touch point, we need to say that we are going to offer a paid product as well. Then, give a limited window of opportunity (maybe 3 to 5 days) for your subscribers to buy your course.

I learned the concepts of launching a course. I launched one course, and that too only once. I did not get good results.

Then I found Ryan Deiss. I bought few courses from DigitalMarketer and enrolled in their membership package that taught how to optimize your website for initial offer, upsell, relationship building through emails, driving traffic from Facebook, and a zillion other things.

I was learning and getting some results, but then something stopped me from scaling it up. I always wondered what was the reason behind this.

Was it shiny object syndrome, monkey mind, or lack of focus? Or was something else at play?

Let me share what finally worked for me.

Somewhere amid the above sob story, I learned about Kindle publishing in Amazon. Ryan Lee, a well-known influencer in the online world, partnered with another Kindle publisher to promote a membership program called 6 Figure Kindle Club. I joined to understand the know-how of self-publishing.

I wrote my book and published it as a Kindle eBook. The book was related to public speaking. That's an area I am really passionate about and I just wanted to be helpful for my reader.

When people said that they found it really useful, I felt proud. Then, I created the second book. Followed by the third, then the fourth, and then the fifth.

Slowly, I converted them to paperback, and then into audiobooks. It did not happen in a day. Yes, there was a huge learning curve. I moved on from the membership site to buy other courses, connected with more successful self-published authors such as Steve Scott and Akash Karia, and learned how to launch a book with my bootstrapped budget.

Though it may not sound spectacular, I am proud of the fact that more than 25K (5K paid and 20K free) people have a copy of my work in eBook, paperback, or audiobook format.

For me, it is more than passive income. It is meaning and purpose that I found, which is priceless.

I am not saying that writing books is the best way to create passive income.

Pursue things that you feel *inclined* to. Creating passive income might not be as simple as working for 8 hours a day and getting paid. It is hard, and if anyone says it is easy, they are lying.

If it were easy, everyone would be doing it. And that's why *you* should give it a no-excuses shot. Remember, I told you to save your ego. Use it to create passive income. It's absolutely worth it.

Right now, you may be comfortable where you are but you never know when the storm will hit. I believe the disruption has already started in the tech world, and that's a more compelling reason why you should pursue the path of passive income.

If you are interested in any topic for creating passive income, you'll get plenty of options. However, there are many money suckers out there. Just be absolutely sure about the credibility of the course, and the source. Check if the source is someone who has been there and done that.

We live in a world where you don't need anybody's permission to do things. Of course, the touch of an influencer or a mentor can create wonders. But, all I am saying is that you don't need to wait for anybody's approval for doing useful things.

Technology companies have changed the rules of the game by giving a platform for common people. Amazon allows you to advertise and sell physical products, eBooks, paperback books, or audiobooks. Apple allows you to create apps and sell in their platform. Google allows people to find you, and you can advertise to the whole world. Facebook allows you to advertise to any demographic in any part of the world. Udemy allows you to create and sell courses in their platform.

Yes, everything has a learning curve. But what I am trying to say is that the *facility* and *opportunity* are there. You just need to do some hard work.

If you want to get started, you just need to answer two questions. Everything just boils down to these two simple questions:

- Who will your idea (product or a service) serve?

- Will they open their wallet and pay?

That's it.

To find an answer for the first question, think about why people should pay you.

People pay and recommend only those things that add value to their life. Think about how your idea can add value to someone's life. In other words, think about how your idea can solve people's problems.

No one can answer the second question, because there are a lot of factors that govern why someone will spend money. To remove this unpredictability, the best option is to *test* the idea. Test the idea on a very small scale. If it works, that's good. If it fails, that's good too. You'll at least know what not to do, and save lots of time.

You can literally build a website, create a minimum viable product (or service) for your idea, and drive targeted traffic to check if your target audience is ready to pay for your idea. The entire setup can be built using free trials offered by various SAAS (software as a service) solutions out there in the market. You might need to spend some money for traffic, but it won't create a hole in your pocket. Once things seem to work, you can invest in long-term setup of website, email service provider, shopping cart, traffic, and other infrastructure setup.

There will be work, lots of work. But it's learnable. And as a techie, it should certainly be learnable. After all, it's a technology thing!

If you want to know the best resources and tools out there, download the cheat sheet, which is current, at <u>www.publicspeakKing.com/coast.</u>

I have realized that there are literally hundreds of "how to do" resources available on almost any topic in this world. Knowing "what to do" is where you need to do some researching, and soul searching.

But there is one major obstacle, which is engulfing everyone like plague. That's why I dedicated the final chapter as an antidote, so that you take a path that leads to meaning and purpose.

KEY TAKEAWAYS

- Getting a good job is not the goal. A job will give us decent money but will not make us financially independent.

- Buy things based on needs rather than wants. Declutter and let go stuff that you are not using. Spend premium on things you need, and be cutthroat on things you don't need.

- *Automate* savings by doing a direct debit on payday.

- Clear your credit card debt. Reduce your mortgage payment. This will free up your mind to do creative things.

- Reduce your taxes by talking to a good financial adviser. Simple options include non-taxable expenses and tax-saving investments.

- An asset will help you generate money and its monetary value may increase over time. Liabilities will suck money out of you and their monetary value may decrease over time. Invest your time, money, and energy in creating assets. Assets generate passive income.

- To create passive income, pursue ideas that you feel *inclined* to. Find an audience who will benefit from your idea. Using a minimum budget and infrastructure setup, test whether the audience will open their wallets and pay.

CHAPTER 12

FIVE KEYS TO UNLOCK YOUR
CREATIVE POTENTIAL

*In which, we'll see: creator versus consumer, what Robert Frost missed in
The Road Not Taken, why rejections are good, how to find a good mentor,
why it is sometimes good to give up goals, why WHAT is more important
than HOW*

The whole world wants your attention. Attention has become
a precious commodity. And there is a reason for this. We are
in the midst of a consumer wave, which is affecting us like
plague.

How do you think Google, Facebook, Twitter, Amazon, Apple have
become billion-dollar brands within a quick time frame?

I am not against them. In fact, I am a big fan of these companies.
But, I want to point out that they were successful in catching the
consumer wave that is sweeping this whole world.

Slowly, without any active thought, we are turning out to be diehard
consumers.

As a result, our mindset is like, "Why bother to do anything creative
when we can have so much with little effort?"

- It's easy to read a book while it is hard to write one.

- It's easy to watch a YouTube video while it is hard to create one.

- It's easy to buy things while it is hard to sell things.

Consuming things is easy. Creating things is hard. There is no denying that fact. It is supposed to be hard and that's why only a few create things while the masses consume things. But here's the spoiler against consumers. By and large, consumers spend money and creators make money.

You can continue to be a consumer or choose to be a creator, which is the antidote to the consumer wave.

One deterrent is that the world seems to go beyond our control. With globalization, no individual seems empowered to tackle the social, economic, and environment problems. That does not mean that we attempt less to lower our chances of failure.

Being a techie, I should not say this but technology has made it worse. Hasn't it?

Don't we feel, "It is my right to have the information and commodities at my fingertips and I can consume whenever I want"?

If we are not careful, this consumerist approach will kill the creator within us. You may ignore this feeling for a while and then forget about it altogether. Then, work will become mechanical. You might get depressed, not knowing that the true reason is that you were ignoring your creative potential.

Your desire to do things, and the emotional connect, is what will help you find things you like to create for yourself.

Before it is too late, prep yourself to create things. It's high time to take that damn decision.

1. Take quick decision

When I was in fifth grade, I came across the poem *The Road Not Taken* by Robert Frost. If you haven't heard this poem, here's the gist:

Robert Frost is caught at a crossroads where he has to make a decision. One road seems to be taken by many people. The other seems to be taken by few. He regrets that he may not be able to come back and take the other road, but he took the road less traveled and said that it made all the difference.

After reading the poem, everybody wants to explore new avenues. Robert said that taking the road less traveled made all the difference. But, he never said he was successful because he took that road less traveled. Robert might have been just as successful if he had taken the road more traveled.

But here's the thing. He might have not been successful at all if he had been standing at the crossroads thinking forever whether taking *the road less traveled* was the right decision.

Robert never said that taking that damn decision as quickly as possible is absolutely important. I am saying that it is important. Not just at work, in fact, this is more important in life.

You might want to write a book or start a blog or learn a new technology or learn public speaking or learn to play an instrument. Are you saying, "I'll start writing a book when I have some more time" or "I'll start exercising starting next month when my project becomes less hectic"?

Not just you, even I have been a big victim of postponing decisions in the hope that I'll get a perfect answer later. The problem is that it seldom happens. Even if it happens, it's not worth it because you lost so much time. Two weeks from now, or two months from now, if there is no new information that will help you to make a better decision, then the decision you *make now is the best decision.*

One way or another, making the decision is Important. This is so vital. There is a myth that people who have done cool things like creating a world-class product or a world-class company or a great career did it because they took all the right decisions.

They did not take all the right decisions.

They took quick decisions and moved on. They learned what worked and kept tuning their decision-making process.

Steve Jobs, one of the pioneers in the tech industry, might be a perfect example.

Jeffrey S. Young notes in his book *Steve Jobs, the Journey Is the Reward*, that Jobs was not interested in business or electronics as a student. He took calligraphy classes. He walked barefoot and wore his hair long. He ate food at Hare Rama Hare Krishna Center. He grew tired of being broke and moved back to his parents' home in California. He got into a night-shift job at Atari because the ad said, "Have fun and make money." Then, he left that job to visit India to explore his spiritual side!

After Steve Jobs returned from India, his friend Steve Wozniak called Jobs for some business help. It was here that Jobs got in touch with the tech world. Jobs pitched Wozniak about the idea of selling circuit boards. Then, one day a reputable computer store said that they didn't want circuit boards but fully assembled computers. Jobs just jumped on the opportunity. Wozniak and Jobs arranged some money, assembled full computers, and Apple was born.

Let's study this story for a minute.

Jobs dropped out of college. That's still okay. If there is fire in your belly to start a world-class company, you can drop out of college, right?

No, that's not what happened.

He dropped out of college, and took a calligraphy class. He did not even get a proper job. He took a job because the ad said, "Have fun and make money." And then he quit and suddenly went to India!

These are not the decisions that one expects in the résumé of a pioneer who built one of the most powerful tech companies in the world.

We should learn something here, right? After all, Steve Jobs did it. I would not advise doing any of what he did except learning to make that damn decision and move on.

And even Steve Jobs meant the same when he said, "You can't connect the dots looking forward. You can only connect them looking backwards. So you have to trust that the dots will somehow connect in your future. You have to trust in something—your gut, destiny, life, karma, whatever. This approach has never let me down, and it has made all the difference in my life."[1]

When I look back, I can connect the dots. I did not have the slightest thought of writing books. But competing in speech contests helped me improve my writing skills. For these contests, we need to spend hundreds of hours writing, rewriting, and polishing the speech scripts. It was that damn decision to compete in the contests that equipped my writing skills. And being a software techie helped with computer typing skills!

We all postpone things and get caught up in thoughts like, "When I become confident, I'll go ask that girl for a date" or "When I become successful, I'll be happy." In fact, I found the above to be opposite.

When I asked a girl for a date, I became more confident. When I chose to be happy, I felt more successful. So, when you are caught in the crossroads, make that damn decision to enter either one. When you decide to enter, you commit to that thing and stick with it.

One of the major blocks to a quick decision is that we fear that we may face rejections. That's why we need to play the numbers game.

2. Play the numbers game

When was the first time you faced a major rejection? I remember. The fast-growing tech company CTS rejecting me in the interview was kind of big for me. Then, then India's largest tech company TCS rejected me (looks like my stars were not aligned with the letters C, T, and S). It was more painful than getting rejected by a beautiful girl.

Rejection is often counted in the context of work or relationships. If you hadn't realized, it's there everywhere.

When a beautiful girl ignores you and talks to the guy next to you, that's rejection. When you ask a close friend for feedback on your book, and you don't get any response, that's rejection. When you make your move to have sex, and your spouse says, "No, baby," that's rejection.

When you expect things from others, you also invite rejection. That's life.

If somebody told that you are too sensitive to take rejections, that's crap. Rejections are painful. Even small rejections are painful. And that's why we need to *develop thick skin.*

You know who inspires me to develop a thick skin?

A buffalo. Seriously. I love buffalos. In sun, rain, or sludge, a buffalo has the coolest look. I feel it says, "Just chill."

And I believe this is an essential quality that every techie, heck every person, needs to develop.

Thick skin not only protects you from rejection but also from idiots who might confront you for unnecessary reasons.

I might have depressed you by telling you need to develop thick skin towards rejection. But I am also going to inspire you. Though you'll face many rejections, you will hear an occasional "Yes" as well. Trust me on this.

Some call it the law of averages. I like to call it the *numbers game*, and the one who knows how to play this game, wins. Here's the beauty about rejections. Only when you ask for things that can be rejected, will you get things that are worthy.

As Tim Ferriss, author of *The Four-Hour Work Week,* rightly said, "A person's success in life can usually be measured by the number of uncomfortable conversations he or she is willing to have."

A few years ago, I wrote *Toastmaster's Secret,* which is a practical know-how book for the first 10 speeches someone will take in their journey in Toastmasters. I really believed in it and that gave me the confidence to send it to five World Champions of Public Speaking, asking for a testimonial. When I think about it now, it's a big ASK.

Just so that you know, it was not a cold pitch. I had interaction with them at least through email or bought some of their coaching programs earlier. But, they were not obligated to help me—a first-time author.

And that's exactly what happened. One month passed, nobody replied. Two months passed, nobody replied. Three passed, nobody replied. But after four months, I got a reply from Lance Miller with a testimonial. He was the 2005 World Champion of Public Speaking.

Boy, I was excited.

Let me share another experience where I contacted world-class experts with whom I did not have any prior connection. I sent out a genuine email to 16 people whose TED talks are currently the *most viewed TED talks*. I asked if they'd share their thoughts for an upcoming book project.

How many do you think responded?

Ten responded. Five said YES and eventually answered my questions. Five respectfully said NO and gave reasons for saying so.

And the positive replies came from world-class experts such as Daniel H. Pink, Simon Sinek, Julian Treasure, Dr. Jill Bolte Taylor, and Pamela Meyer.

This happened because of the numbers game. Out of 16, six did not respond, five said YES, five said NO. If you think that this is a mediocre response, it's not.

You'll know when you do a similar activity. Actually, this is a pretty high rate of response. Maybe they trusted me because of my earlier book projects related to public speaking. Maybe they realized that I am serious about my stuff. Whatever the reason, I felt proud that five world-class experts having the most viewed TED talks said YES to my cold pitch.

Here's what you need to understand and this is really important. If people say NO or don't respond, most of the time the reason is not you or your work.

They are just BUSY.

Sometimes, what you ask might not be interesting to them. We don't need to overanalyze the reasons.

Ask one person. If it's a NO, *move to the next one*, then the next one. Ask 10, at least one might say YES. Here's another thing. If you ask a hundred (just an exaggerated figure) people and no one is saying YES, then there could be a problem with your request.

It's all about: Are you trustable? Are you giving a good reason? Are you adding value? Show these things in your request, and your chance of getting a YES will become high.

For example, go talk to the girl (or guy) who is in your crush list. I'm not telling you to be aggressive. Be respectful and just talk. If you connect, ask her to go for a coffee. Just make a simple move. Most probably she'll say NO and that's okay. It'll sting. It will hurt your ego. But be patient. Save your ego when it matters (such as creating passive income). Not for now. Now, you are undergoing rejection training.

Go ask the next one. You might not believe me but you'll be far more confident because you are better prepared for a NO. And that confidence will shine through when you ask the next time, where you might land a YES. And it'll be absolutely worth it.

This concept is very powerful, and it also works like crazy. Now, that you know the numbers game, let's talk about finding someone who can help you to play a better game.

3. Find a good mentor

Your chances of learning anything in this world are much better with a mentor. Having a mentor helps you in a lot of ways.

That's why it is necessary to have a mentor at your workplace, especially when you are new. I was very fortunate to have a good mentor at the start of my career. Everything was new to me. The way things work. The technology. The people. The culture. The language. I used to bug my mentor with a lot of questions. But because I was sincere and willing to learn, she was happy to help me. I still owe that initial know-how in the tech world to my mentor.

At that time, I did not even know the power of a mentor. I was like, "Well, it's the workplace. People are supposed to help. I am obligated to get help."

It was when I ventured to learn public speaking skills and started participating in contests that I realized the power of a good mentor.

A mentor can advise you on what is right, what is wrong. More importantly, a mentor says what the *exact next step* is.

In August 2011, sitting in the third floor of the Atrium building at Aetna, I did a Google search for "Champion Speakers in Connecticut."

Just to give you some background, at that time, I was crazy or to sound decent, extremely passionate... I don't know which. I devoured every tip, technique, article, DVD, CD. If any World Champion of Public Speaking was saying something, I'd think, "I have to implement it." I realized that too much energy without proper channelization was harming rather than helping me.

I badly needed a good mentor.

Google search completed in microseconds and the results showed up. All the links pointed to Jerry Aiyathurai. He seemed to have given a TEDx speech in Simsbury, Connecticut. I checked out his TEDx talk and I loved it. Google helped me find Jerry Aiyathurai! Sometimes technology is really awesome. I love Google. I love technology.

I chalked out a plan: I'll find some places where Jerry visits. I'll go there and do my best so that there is a chance that Jerry will notice me. Before you judge me further, I'll tell you what exactly happened.

I went to the forum in Berlin, Connecticut. It was Central Connecticut Advanced Toastmasters Club, where Jerry visits on a weekly basis.

On that day, a senior member gave a speech. I made sure I gave the best feedback. After the meeting, I went up to Jerry and said, "Hi." He said, "Well, your evaluation was great."

I'm thinking, "Yay." We spoke for more than an hour and that was our first meeting.

Listen, I already had a good understanding of public speaking and had already won half a dozen contests. However, I was truly amazed with the insights. It just blew me away. I felt like I did not know anything about public speaking.

I'm proud to say this. It was his teachings, mentoring, and guidance that really helped me. It was that relationship which took my public speaking skills to the next level.

You might ask, "How do you find a good mentor?"

Good question.

If you have a relationship with someone who is good at something that you are looking to learn, ask that person. This can be paid or free. Talking about "free," I believe nothing is free in this world. It is better to give something in return. Maybe it could be a promise to pass on the learning or something else. Think. Think.

If you do not have a relationship with someone, here are some ways to start building one.

- Read their books and strike a genuine conversation in an email or in any other communication channel such as social media, or blog.

- If they haven't written books, buy their programs or courses to get access to them.

- Apply their ideas and let them know about your results. It'll thrill them.

- Appear in person and strike up a conversation at a common forum.

Learning from mentors has changed the way I see things. It is a good idea to have one in any area of life that you want to improve.

When I got stuck during the book publishing process, I searched for one. I found Derek Doepkar, who became my publishing coach. And that's one of the main reasons why my last few books hit #1 Amazon bestseller in a few subcategories.

Keep looking for one. When the student is ready, the master appears.

4. Master one thing

When I was a kid, I wanted to become good at everything I saw. And you know what happened—I did not become good at anything. And being born in a typical middle-class family, my dad told me to do anything as long as it was related to my school exams.

Things have changed a lot now. These days, I see parents throttle their kids with loads of activities related to sports or art or other skills. That's not good either.

If you are still in your 20s, or early 30s, or whatever age actually, stop doing activities that do not matter to you. I'd recommend that you just focus on any one thing and get really good at it. It does not have to be related to some new technology, but that's okay as long as you have an inclination.

It could also be skills such as copy writing, one-to-one selling, speaking on stage, speaking on webinars, writing books, creating apps, painting, craftwork, networking, photography, or any other skill that enables *you to transfer value*. There is a catchphrase "Jack of all trades but master of none." You should aim to be a Jack-of-all-trades but master of one.

This one thing is not a lifelong thing. We just need to *focus on one thing at a time*. But there will be objections. And we might feel guilty of not achieving the one thing because of objections. And that's why, though it is controversial, I want to share this secret of *giving up certain goals.*

Let me explain this further.

It was a revelation for me and I can't wait to share with you. Have you felt guilty when you give up on goals? I have. But not anymore because I'm going to share a secret which can guide us to decide if giving up on the goals is OK or not.

It's the concept of low-level vs. medium-level vs. high-level goals, which I learned from the book *Grit* by Angela Duckworth.

This high-level goal is our *one thing* we want to focus on. For example, I want to go to New York from Atlanta. I'll use this example of reaching a place because it is relatable and helps us to see this concept in action.

1. A high-level goal is what you want, your one thing at the moment. In this case, reaching New York.

2. A medium-level goal is how you'll achieve high-level goals. In this case, take a flight.

3. A low-level goal is how you'll achieve your medium-level goals. In this case, book your flight with Delta Airlines.

Now, the strategy is: It is *OK to give up or change* your low-level goals, it is *NOT OK to give up but it is OK to change* medium-level goals, but it is *NOT OK to give up or change* your high-level goals.

The resistance to give up or change goals should increase as the goal type increases.

For instance, let's talk about giving up or changing the low-level goal in the above scenario. If there is no ticket on Delta Airlines, you can book your flight with another carrier. It doesn't hurt as long as the flight takes you to New York, right?

Now, let's talk about changing a medium-level goal. If you do not get a flight on any airline, there is an option to use a car. It still does not hurt as long as you reach New York, right?

But, here's the kicker. You cannot and should not change your high-level goals, which is your one thing. I mean would you go to Chicago just because the tickets available on Delta were for Chicago? You wouldn't.

Personally, I used to feel guilty when I gave up certain goals and moved on to the next goal. Remember how I hopped from platform to platform: affiliate marketing, YouTube, Udemy, book publishing, and whatnot.

It all started making sense why I should not feel guilty about it. My high-level goal was to earn passive income by helping people with public speaking skills. As long as I am helping people learn public speaking skills through my books, my high-level goal is met, which is my one thing. It does not matter which platform I use or how I am doing it because these are my medium-level goals.

Now, let's talk about two high-level goals.

For example, becoming good at public speaking as well as becoming good at writing books. That's overwhelming. If you ask me to do it together, I might not. Even now, when any current book project is on, I don't participate in speech contests.

Earlier, my high-level goal—one thing—was public speaking. Now, the high-level goal—new one thing—is writing books. But, I am able to leverage the speech writing skills to write books. Though there is a difference, I am able to handle it.

It makes more sense now, but I did not realize this earlier. When you become a master of one thing at a time, you keep adding that skill to your earlier skills and compound that knowledge to produce good work.

I'll not sugarcoat this: Becoming good at any skill is hard. It needs passion and perseverance. But as Tom Hanks, playing the role of Jimmy Dugan in the movie *A League of Their Own*, brilliantly said, "It's supposed to be hard. If it wasn't hard, everyone would do it. That hard is what makes it great."

In order to unlock creative potential, we learned about taking quick decisions, playing the numbers game, finding a good mentor, mastering one thing at a time, and now let's see the final key, which is probably the first thing you need to do after reading this book.

5. Find your WHAT

Many start with questions such as, "Who am I?" "Why should I?" "How should I?" But I believe the central question we need to ask, and find an answer to, should be:

What do I want?

I've struggled with this question a lot. So I dabbled with different things. One secret that has helped me to find the WHAT is to ask whether what I want is EXCITING.

Nobody around you will talk about excitement as a useful emotion. Hence you may feel it is short-lived and rare. Chances are that people around you are not excited. Or they get excited at the wrong time and for the wrong reason. That's why you don't feel it often, and even when you feel it, you dismiss it because it's not common. Complaining, gossiping, negativity, or mediocrity seems to be common. Hence, without us knowing, we get caught up being common.

Excitement is such a precious thing. Think about it. We take action when we are excited. That's why it is absolutely necessary to be excited about what you want to do.

It's not like, "Yeah." It's like, "Hell, yeah."

Find what excites you—whether in your personal life, at work or any side hustle that you want to do. What you start off might not be the right thing. But it will lead you to other things. And eventually you'll find what you love to do.

If the excitement test is not your thing, ask yourself, "Will I be proud of doing this?" Being proud of something you do is a really good feeling. Embrace this feeling. It is a shortcut for finding things you want to do.

Again, don't worry about HOW. HOW can always be figured out. There is more than enough information, and more than enough people who are already successful in what you want to do.

You never know how tomorrow will turn out. Start small. Start with just with one thing that matters to you. Now.

Finally, in the conclusion to this book, I'd like to share my take on the two most used, rather misused, words in life.

KEY TAKEAWAYS

- Attention has become scarce. Be a creator, not a consumer.

- Take quick decisions. See what works, and connect the dots later.

- Develop thick skin towards rejections.

- Play the numbers game. Ask more people for help, and a few will say yes.

- Find a good mentor. A mentor can shortcut your path to reach your goals.

- Do one thing at a time.

- You can give up or change low-level goals. You cannot give up but you can change medium-level goals. You should not change high-level goals.

- To find what you want to do, see if it is exciting, or ask if you'll be proud of doing it.

CONCLUSION

If you are reading this book, you have a desire to get better, to change your life for the better.

I want to tell you about something that helped me change my views about those two important words, "success" and "failure."

I always classified things as a success or a failure.

- I got first rank in my class, I am a success.

- If girls did not look at me, I am a failure.

- I got into the best college, I am a success.

- I got rejected in an interview, I am a failure.

- I got selected in an interview, I am a success.

- I score low marks in MBA entrance, I am a failure.

- I win a contest, I am a success.

- A girl rejects me, I am a failure.

- I get promoted, I am a success.

- My code breaks in production, I am a failure.

- I get an appreciation, I am a success.

- I get an escalation, I am a failure.

- I get the best performance rating, I am a success.

It was a big moment for me when I realized that the above approach was WRONG.

In fact, being a techie helped me. I knew that Windows and Mac OS are undeniably the most dominant operating systems for decades. Though there are breakthrough technological advances happening, they are still dominant. Despite their past success or failures, they keep releasing new versions. The reason is simple. They are a *work in progress.*

When I looked around, the things that were stable and durable were all built on this philosophy. And that philosophy is to be a work in progress. Be it a person, a company, or a nation, the ones who were making a mark were those that were a work in progress.

This thought was fascinating. In fact, it was liberating. It just took the pressure off me to feel like a success or a failure.

A few years ago, I got a wacky idea of writing a book. After doing some homework, I realized that I had everything I needed to start off: a computer and excitement to write. The rest such as how to edit, format, publish and sell, seemed to be figure-out-able. I self-published my first book. What happened?

Nothing happened. Only a few books sold.

But, I worked on a better title, a better description, better cover, and I saw some sales. Is that a success? I don't know. But I know this. I am a work in progress.

So, I wrote another book with the learning from my earlier book project. Better results. And I wrote another book with the learning from my earlier projects. Even better. Before I knew it, I completed five books.

As I am writing this sixth book of mine, I have got so many emails from so many amazing people on how my books have helped them.

To me that is priceless.

That's the power of this philosophy. It changed my life and can change yours because you can go to places where you have never been.

And that's my earnest desire: **to help you unlock your real potential, so that you can live a life with purpose, and meaning.**

I have learned that being coachable is one of the key traits of a winner. You have shown that trait by reading this book.

However, I want to tell you that *knowing* is just one thing, *applying* your knowledge in ways that matter is another.

In fact, it is the main thing. If you apply the learning, I promise you that it'll change the way you function. You probably won't be able to incorporate all the things at one go. However, when you take one thing at a time, you'll see the results for yourself.

And that's when I'll be thrilled.

If you want to share any feedback, stories, or experiences, feel free to reach me at Rama@publicspeakKing.com. I'll be excited to hear from you.

If this book was helpful, you can share your thoughts with other readers by writing a review in Amazon.

Thank you very much. You have been an awesome reader.

Keep Smiling, Keep Rocking, and Happy Working!

Wish You Success,

Ramakrishna Reddy

BONUS. VALUE-ADD

First off, thank you for taking the time to read and finish this book.

You could have spent your money and time to do many other things. But you chose this book.

As an expression of gratitude and to follow my own advice of adding more value, I want to offer you something more. I have put together valuable resources that can really help you further. I intend to keep this place updated so that resources are current.

- Current online tools and resources to test your product or idea

- Customizable PowerPoint template that shows the design principles in action

- Speech templates for giving informational and persuasive speeches

Visit: http://publicspeakking.com/coast/

ACKNOWLEDGMENTS

This project would not have been possible if Infosys had not given me a chance to enter the technology world. Thank you for giving me the ticket to become a techie.

My initial mentors: Prajakta Khatavkar and Ashwin Lobo your guidance in those first few years was invaluable. A friendly shout to all my friends who worked in Legacy claims project, Legacy Rocks!

My superiors: Shubhada Gopale, Vimal Rupani, Dharmesh Dhruve, Haresh Khemani, Rohit Mahajan, Amrish Raje, Swati Mundra, Shalaka Borkar, Jigar Mehta, Rohini Pulliwar, Amol Mulik, Armindo Jorge, Roy Carcia, Randy Pence, Alfred Garbanolla, Jagjit Singh Ajmani, Kapil Bhaid, Raghavendra Rao, Vasudeo Rane, and Vikram Masur, Craig Bryant, Fortunato Giovana, Ana B. Chavez, Alicia Lemos, Annette Eaton, Pawara Kim, Tyler Singley. You all taught me so much about work that no one person, book, or course could ever teach.

All my colleagues, subordinates, toastmasters, school and college buddies: you are the very reason how I shaped myself. You know who you are, I don't want to mention names and miss out on anyone. Thank you for coming into my life.

Coming on to creation of this book project, I want to thank TD Arun, Mohan Raj, Senthil Kumar, Arun Prabhu Vijayan, Balaji Kalaimani, Rahul Dolia, Arulkumar VB, and Mythili Devarajulu for spending time, giving me inputs, and sharing useful feedback. This helped me in keeping what mattered, and removing what did not matter.

I want to thank my wife, Priyanka Marcus, for being really patient while I was working on this project. You also gave me tons of inputs, some knowingly and some unknowingly. You are awesome. Thank you so much, Jindu. I love you.

I want to thank my dad, Narayana Reddy, and sisters—Leelavathy, Lakshmi, and Indumathy—for the blessings and constant support that you all give in whatever I want to pursue. Thank you for caring for me after the loss of mom. I am so lucky to be born in this family.

I want to thank my mom Ammayeammal, who is also my guardian angel. Mom—I am working with computers. I hit the keyboard and money keeps falling in my bank account. I miss you, and I love you.

I also want to thank Aaniyah Ahmed from 99designs.com for helping me design a beautiful book cover. The amount of iterations that I asked for would irritate even the most patient designer. Thank you for being calm and cool.

I want to thank the advance readers of this book. I owe you a big hug for the thoughts and feedback. Thank you for being kind and supportive.

Finally, I want to thank my editor Marcia Abramson for agreeing to grow with this project. Despite of your mom's loss, you supported this project. I have no words to express my gratitude. You define professionalism for me. Thank you once again.

Notes on Sources

Chapter 1

You are an owner

John. G. Miller, *The Question Behind the Question* (TarcherPerigee, 2004)

Failure is not an option

(1) BR Srikanth, "Poor test result drives Infosys techie to suicide," April 2009 for Hindustan Times
http://www.hindustantimes.com/india/poor-test-result-drives-infosys-techie-to-suicide/story-6s7vp5nvBF8jqEd23znhCJ.html

Sticking longer is not loyalty

(2) Matthew Sturdevant, "Aetna Laying Off 160, Mainly Managers In Innovation, Technology and Service Operations," October 2012 for the *Hartford Courant*
http://articles.courant.com/2012-10-02/news/hc-aetna-layoffs-20121002_1_health-exchange-aetna-spokeswoman-cynthia-michener-aetna-employees

The only thing that matters at work

(3) Dawn Kawamoto, "Apple acquires Next, Jobs," December 1996 for cnet.com
https://www.cnet.com/news/apple-acquires-next-jobs/

(4) James Mann, "Why Narendra Modi Was Banned From the U.S." May 2014 for the *Wall Street Journal*
https://www.wsj.com/articles/why-narendra-modi-was-banned-from-the-u-s-1399062010

Chapter 2

Boss

Daniel H. Pink, *Drive* (Riverhead Books, 2011)

Customers

Anna Durai speech, "No need to be a marketing expert to understand customer value," published in YouTube by official TEDxtalks channel
https://www.youtube.com/watch?v=g_Flojqd_-M

Office politics

Robert Greene, *Mastery* (Penguin Books, 2012)

Chapter 3

(1) Parkinson's Law from Wikipedia
https://en.wikipedia.org/wiki/Parkinson%27s_law

Multitasking

(2) John Naish, "Is multi-tasking bad for your brain? Experts reveal the hidden perils of juggling too many jobs," August 2009 for dailymail.co.uk
http://www.dailymail.co.uk/health/article-1205669/Is-multi-tasking-bad-brain-Experts-reveal-hidden-perils-juggling-jobs.html

(3) "Infomania worse than marijuana," April 2005 for news.bbc.co.uk
http://news.bbc.co.uk/2/hi/uk_news/4471607.stm

Priority should be priority

Stephen R. Covey, *The 7 Habits of Highly Effective People* (Simon & Schuster, 2013)

All hours are not the same

(4) Andrew Trotman, "Facebook's Mark Zuckerberg: Why I wear the same T-shirt every day," November 2014 for telegraph.co.uk http://www.telegraph.co.uk/technology/facebook/11217273/ Facebooks-Mark-Zuckerberg-Why-I-wear-the-same-T-shirt-every-day.html

(5) Michael Lewis, "Obama's Way," October 2012 for vanityfair.com http://www.vanityfair.com/news/2012/10/michael-lewis-profile-barack-obama

Insight from Vilfredo Pareto

(6) Pareto principle from Wikipedia https://en.wikipedia.org/wiki/Pareto_principle

Process is not the thing

(7) Jeff Bezos annual letter to employees https://www.sec.gov/Archives/edgar/ data/1018724/000119312517120198/d373368dex991.htm

Simple tools and strategies

Atul Gawande, *Checklist Manifesto* (Metropolitan Books, 2009)

(8) Pam A. Mueller and Daniel M Oppenheimer, "The Pen Is Mightier Than the Keyboard: Advantages of Longhand Over Laptop Note Taking," Volume 25, Issue 6, 2014. *Association for Psychological Science* http://journals.sagepub.com/doi/abs/10.1177/0956797614524581

Chapter 6

(1), (2) Malcom Gladwell podcast interview, "Malcolm Gladwell Interview (Full Episode) | The Tim Ferriss Show (Podcast),"

published in YouTube by official Tim Ferriss Channel
https://www.youtube.com/watch?v=vrBEbgnG01s

Create a slide deck that doesn't suck

(3) Jo Mackiewicz, "Audience Perceptions of Fonts in Projected
PowerPoint Text Slides," November 2016 for **International
Professional Comm**unication Conference, 2006 IEEE
https://www.researchgate.net/publication/224059845_Audience_
Perceptions_of_Fonts_in_Projected_PowerPoint_Text_Slides

Chapter 7

How to be more innovative

(1) Jim Avery, "How Xerox Invented the Information Age (and Gave
it Away)," October 2010 for cracked.com
http://www.cracked.com/article_18807_how-xerox-invented-
information-age-and-gave-it-away.html

Austin Kleon, *Steal Like an Artist* (Workman Publishing, 2012)

Dialogue from *Viral Loop: From Facebook to Twitter, How Today's
Smartest Businesses Grow Themselves* by Adam L. Penenberg
(Hyperion, 2009)

(2) "Robert Kearns#Intermittent wipers" published in Wikipedia
https://en.wikipedia.org/wiki/Robert_Kearns#Intermittent_wipers

Chapter 8

Becoming emotional

(1) Tony Robbins's speech, "Why we do what we do," February
2006 at TEDGlobal, Monterey, California
https://www.ted.com/talks/tony_robbins_asks_why_we_do_what_
we_do

(2) Robert Waldinger's speech, "What makes a good life? Lessons from the longest study on happiness," November 2015 at TEDxBeaconStreet
https://www.ted.com/talks/robert_waldinger_what_makes_a_good_life_lessons_from_the_longest_study_on_happiness/

Robert Greene, *Mastery* (Penguin Books, 2012)

Chapter 9

The power of habits

Gary Keller and Jay Papasan, The One Thing (Bard Press, July 2013)

Charles Duhigg, The Power of Habit (Random House, 2012)

How to handle stress

(1) Ullrich Wagner et al., "Sleep Inspires Insight," January 2004 for *Nature* 427

www.nature.com/nature/journal/v427/n6972/full/nature02223.html

https://www.ncbi.nlm.nih.gov/pubmed/14737168 (US National Library of Medicine, National Institute of Health)

(2) Kelly McGonigal speech, "How to make stress your friend," June 2013 at TEDGlobal
https://www.ted.com/talks/kelly_mcgonigal_how_to_make_stress_your_friend

Chapter 10

Dr. Sue Johnson, *Hold Me Tight* (Hachette Book Group, 2008)

What women want

John Gray, *Men Are from Mars, Women Are from Venus* (HarperCollins, 2009)

Let's talk about sex

Napoleon Hill, *Think and Grow Rich* (Random House, 1960)

How to handle fights

(1) "Transactional analysis" published in Wikipedia
https://en.wikipedia.org/wiki/Transactional_analysis

Dr. Sue Johnson, *Hold Me Tight* (Hachette Book Group, 2008)

Chapter 11

Embrace frugality

Greg McKeown, *Essentialism* (Crown Business, 2014)

Manage money suckers

(1) IRS Withholding Calculator and sample W4 form
https://www.irs.gov/individuals/irs-withholding-calculator

(2) Kevin Bonsor and Dave Roos, "How Income Taxes Work" for
howstuffworks.com
http://money.howstuffworks.com/personal-finance/personal-
income-taxes/income-tax.htm

Ramit Sethi, *I Will Teach You to Be Rich* (Workman Publishing
Company, 2009)

Ashwin Sanghi and Sunil Dalal, *13 Steps to Bloody Good Wealth*
(Westland, 2016)

Invest in assets

Robert T. Kiyosaki, *Rich Dad Poor Dad* (Plata Publishing, 2015)

(3) Mark Cuban interview, "Mark Cuban: Only Morons Start a Business on a Loan," published in YouTube by official Bloomberg Channel
https://www.youtube.com/watch?v=KYneLGRTgy8

Chapter 12

Take quick decision

Jeffrey S. Young, *Steve Jobs, the Journey is the Reward* (1988)

(1) Steve Jobs speech, 2005 Stanford Commencement Address, published in YouTube by official Stanford University Channel
https://www.youtube.com/watch?v=Hd_ptbiPoXM

Master one thing

Angela Duckworth, *Grit* (Scribner, May 2016)

Timothy Ferriss, *The 4-Hour Work Week* (Harmony, November 2009)

Made in the USA
Middletown, DE
10 April 2018